Praise for

How to Listen

"When Oscar Trimboli has something to say about listening, listen. He's the best in the world."
MICHAEL BUNGAY STANIER, bestselling author of
The Coaching Habit and *How to Begin*

"The most powerful leadership tool in my personal and professional life is the power of listening—truly listening to create the most remarkable connection with my family, colleagues, customers, and community partners. *How to Listen* provides valuable insights into how we can strengthen our communication and improve our listening approach in a practical and meaningful way."
NAYSLA EDWARDS, vice president brand, charge cards, & member experience, American Express

"A powerful way to reimagine leadership, this book made me realize how much more we can use listening to build high-performance workplace cultures."
ZOE HAYES, head of B2C marketing, consumer apps, & sport partnerships, AUNZ at Google

"*How to Listen* is the missing piece in executive communications with practical and actionable tips to make us better listeners and, ultimately, better leaders. This book is a must for mastering communication skills in the twenty-first century."
JOANNA STEPHENS KRAMER, head of communications and public affairs, Johnson & Johnson MedTech

"When it comes to designing a strategy, a campaign, or liberating an idea, the most overlooked step is listening. *How to Listen* is a timely reminder of the impact that listening has."
NICOLE TAYLOR, senior vice president and head of LEGO Agency

"Exploring a potent yet overlooked leadership competency, *How to Listen* is a pragmatic addition to an executive library."
STEPHEN JOHNSTON, senior client partner, Korn Ferry

"Oscar Trimboli amazed me by deconstructing how to listen into simple actionable concepts that help my ear see better."
MARIA DEL PILAR MARTIN-MATOS, medical director, Sanofi

"An excellent book that provides practical tips and useful exercises to encourage a conscious effort to improve one's listening skills. Incredibly beneficial for leaders who work across different countries and cultures where there is a need to decode what's unspoken."
STEPHANE ASSELIN, chief executive, Asia, Aurecon

"For a leader and executive, what is the cost of not listening? Trimboli brings to life the opportunity of listening with real stories that resonate alongside pragmatic insights and techniques to practice key skills. Learning how to listen has made the biggest impact on my team, organization, and career."
KERRI-ANNE LORING, executive general manager, business service, Downer

"*How to Listen* creates a pragmatic, professional, and powerful framework to hear what matters before it's too late and very expensive. If you care about ROI, listening is your secret weapon."
OSCAR LEDEZMA, global corporate development & M&A, The Clorox Company

"I will return to *How to Listen* regularly, as I seek to improve and build upon my ability to truly listen. Give yourself the time to internalize Trimboli's valuable insights and the space to practice the helpful exercises and examples. A valuable resource for anyone looking to be a better listener."
SUSAN MCMAHON, CEO, TEDxSydney

"Finally a book that combines the art and science of listening in the workplace. It quickly helped me discover my listening barriers, and I'm now a better leader for my team and customers."
MARC MONDAY, vice president, global strategic partnerships, Sage

"*How to Listen* is the missing piece in the jigsaw puzzle of corporate communication. You can apply its potent and practical techniques immediately whether with the media, investors, or executive teams."
SUSANNAH CLARK, senior vice president, communications, Farfetch

"For board directors, listening is perhaps the most essential skill. No matter how good your listening skills are—and reading *How to Listen* will make you realize that your listening skills aren't necessarily as good as you like to think—Trimboli's insights and practical advice will take your listening to the next level."
JENNIFER LANG, independent non-executive director and actuary

"As a brand owner, listening—to your shoppers, your customers, your associates, and yourself—is critical for your future growth. Trimboli teaches you *how* to listen and most importantly how to *act* on these insights. Transformational!"
GINA HEAD, brand director, Mars

"By far, the best speakers are the best listeners. The definitive book on how to actually improve your listening, *How to Listen* is a fantastic resource to become a more effective leader. Trimboli breaks down what it takes to listen well, learn well, understand better, and empathize more. All critical skills at work and home."
JON YEO, head of curation, TEDxMelbourne

"Based on deep research, *How to Listen* is the lesson we all wish we had in school. Trimboli breaks down the process and allows you to digest it easily. This book could make you a better version of yourself. Buy one, and gift one."

JANE HUXLEY, chief executive officer, ARE Media

"Becoming a great leader is not about you, it's about them. Only when you know how to truly listen to them do you deserve the honor of leading them. This wonderful book will show you how."

SHERILYN SHACKELL, founder & global CEO, The Marketing Academy

discover the hidden key
to better communication

how to listen

oscar trimboli

●● PAGE TWO

Cataloging in publication information is
available from Library and Archives Canada.
ISBN 978-1-77458-191-9 (paperback)
ISBN 978-1-77458-192-6 (ebook)
ISBN 978-1-77458-239-8 (audiobook)

Page Two
pagetwo.com

Edited by Kelly Irving and Amanda Lewis
Cover design by Cameron McKague
Interior design by Jennifer Lum
Interior illustrations by Jeff Winocur
Printed and bound in Canada by Friesens
Distributed in Canada by Raincoast Books
Distributed in the U.S. and internationally by Macmillan

23 24 25 26 5 4 3 2

oscartrimboli.com

To my father,
who lost the use of his tongue from his stroke
and taught me how to listen without words.

contents

Active listeners notice what's said.
Deep listeners explore what isn't said.

your invitation

RITA IS A busy professional with huge responsibilities at home and at work. As the chief operating officer of a publicly traded organization, she always has the monkey on her back, and people are constantly coming to her to solve their problems. It's absolutely exhausting.

She has received multiple awards from business magazines and women's leadership communities and has consistently been at the top of her profession and industry. But she finds leading in these times tough.

She is constantly asking: "Why is coming to work every day like being put into a boxing ring blindfolded, with one arm tied behind my back and three people against me in the ring at the same time?"

Based on the way she has led in the past, Rita thinks that *more* talking, *more* energy, and *faster* communication with others to solve their problems is her way out of back-to-back meetings. She doesn't realize that this Energizer Bunny approach to leadership has ceased to be effective and leaves her feeling drained and disappointed. And it's starting to become evident to her manager.

Rita walks out of her annual performance review with her boss, completely flat with the feedback she has received. She was told that her focus was too far ahead of her peers and team. They feel rushed, interrupted, and like just another problem to be ticked off her list. She was told that she comes across as arrogant, close-minded, quick to judge, and too proud to admit she could be wrong or to acknowledge mistakes.

When she arrives for a team or individual discussion, Rita is physically present yet mentally distant. As a result, the others withdraw and tell her what she wants to hear, because they know she isn't listening. These miscommunications have cost her organization: late projects, defective products, billing errors, a spike in customer complaints, declining profitability, a regulatory investigation, and great employees unexpectedly leaving.

Her manager is clear and direct: "Rita, you have ninety days to adjust your approach. If there is no change from you, then I will need to make the change."

After this meeting, Rita takes the fire stairs to the underground parking lot. She needs the space and time to process what her manager has just said. She had expected a different outcome from her annual performance review, and now she is struggling to make sense of the changes she needs to accomplish. Does she even have a future in this organization?

She jumps into her car and turns on some music—her most inspiring songs. Over the next ten minutes, Rita mentally scrolls through the list of leaders she has always admired, the ones who got the best from her and from others. She fast-forwards through her list: women, men, young, old, work, home, sport, travel, family, and friends.

She asks herself, "Who does this well? Who can I learn from?" In her darkest career moment, two people are in Rita's thoughts: her current manager and the world-champion triathlon coach she had when she was a teenager. Two very different people, in two different roles. What they had in common was their ability to profoundly and deeply listen.

Both listened to what Rita said, yet their superpower was their ability to listen beyond the words. They listened to Rita's energy, her state of mind, and to what she was thinking, not merely saying. They listened to her fears, her aspirations, what she was feeling, and how her actions aligned with her words.

Rita is not isolated or unique in facing these challenges. I have seen a common pattern in the workplace: people believe that the most effective way to communicate and influence someone else is solely through speaking. It is a hard-wired assumption that effective communication is only about how you talk—that being an influential leader is about what you say.

Western society is biased toward heroic and charismatic speakers. If I asked you to name a famous speaker, no doubt you could quickly list them: Winston Churchill, John Kennedy, Eleanor Roosevelt, Martin Luther King, Rosa Parks, and others. If I asked you to name three famous listeners, however, you would struggle. Across roles, industries, organizations, cultures, and countries, there is a prejudice for the speaking leader to be noticed over the listening leader.

Yet there is another way. It is possible to balance speaking and listening to create powerful and influential communicators.

Perhaps you have been in a situation like Rita's. You can remember *that listener* who changed your direction in life.

Listening is a skill,

a strategy, and a practice

—a way to balance how

you communicate

That teacher likely listened deeply to you—your fears and aspirations. They saw your full potential. They heard what was going on for you at that moment: what you felt, said, didn't say, thought, and meant.

Listening is human and intuitive. Listening is the first skill you learned in your mother's womb, at the age of thirty-two weeks—before you could see or speak. Ancient cultures continue to cultivate and teach the wisdom of listening to future generations through the example of their elders.

Listening is a skill, a strategy, and a practice—a way to balance how you communicate. Rather than looking for the one breakthrough idea, or for a one-off tip, trick, or technique, you can improve your listening in every moment and every meeting. Listening is practical, pragmatic, and actionable. All you have to do is focus on being better than you were in your last conversation.

How do I know this? For the last three decades, I have worked with senior leaders at some of the most complex organizations around the globe to help them create:

- Happier customers, clients, citizens, and voters

- Divisions and departments that coordinate their limited resources more effectively

- More engaged and productive employees

- Higher-quality projects and outcomes

- More effective relationships between suppliers, competitors, governments, and regulators

These frameworks, strategies, and practices have emerged from listening with, to, and for people in professional conversations and contexts. Through my consulting, speaking, workshops, webinars, and extensive research over the past thirty years, I have noticed the most significant barriers to listening and what adjustments will make a difference. These barriers emerge before the conversation and during it as your attention wanders.

One of the joys of my work has been leading the Apple Award–winning podcast *Deep Listening*. It's a series of conversations with hundreds of the world's most diverse listeners, from air-traffic controllers and acoustic engineers to body-language experts, deaf and foreign language interpreters, hostage negotiators, journalists, and judges. During these interviews, I have seen a discernible pattern to their listening that reveals what a great listener sounds, looks, and feels like. These shared characteristics of world-class listeners are curiosity, flexibility, and openness.

These interviews changed my approach to listening. Throughout this book, you will be able to listen to these same experts as they highlight a specific skill or mindset they use in their listening during high-stakes discussions. If you would like to practice listening to the interviews I reference after you have finished this book, you can find a link to each one in the Notes section starting on page 265.

In the last decade, I have extensively researched listening through independent research to understand what gets in the way of people's listening. In the chapters to come, I have integrated this evidence about listening barriers and behaviors—collected from over 18,000 people across the globe—to help you understand the art and science of listening.

It's essential to explain the limitations of the research. The information collected does not distinguish the neurotypical or neurodivergent listener. This book is written from the perspective of a neurotypical reader, although we do touch on neurodivergent examples.

I started creating this book not by writing but by listening. Many readers, listeners, and clients challenged me to write a comprehensive book about "how to listen." This listening mindset expanded when I surveyed a range of people who knew me and, more importantly, who didn't to understand what they struggle with when it comes to their listening and what they would like included in such a book.

This work involved over a hundred webinars with groups of fifteen people, in which I listened to their feedback about the structure and contents of this book. I continued to ask for feedback as I wrote each chapter and listened to diverse views during the discussion and the decision on the book title. It was a humbling process to synthesize the perspectives of these people.

Over 2,500 people have been involved in bringing this book to life. Based on their feedback on the title, structure, themes, and stories, I learned and adjusted. The result is a book created with a community.

This community created its name and purpose: the Deep Listening Ambassadors are on a quest to create 100 million Deep Listeners in the world by role-modeling great listening in their workplace.[1]

I'd like to welcome you, as a reader of this book and as someone getting ready to learn about listening, to another place. A place where listening creates more possibilities for you, your career, your family, your friends, and your community. Imagine operating in a world where there are:

- Shorter, more productive meetings

- Fewer mix-ups and misunderstandings

- Healthier relationships at work

- Higher employee trust

- Reduced unnecessary rework

- Sustainable organizations

- Opportunities to think, hear, and see your most complex challenges differently

There are Five Levels of Listening, each of which requires the foundation of the previous level. This book will take you through each level in order:

Yourself: Get Ready to Listen & Give and Pay Attention (chapters 2 & 3)

Content: Hear, See, and Sense (chapter 4)

Context: Explore the Backstory & Notice How It Is Said (chapters 5 & 6)

Unsaid: Focus On What Is Unsaid (chapter 7)

Meaning: Listen for Their Meaning (chapter 8)

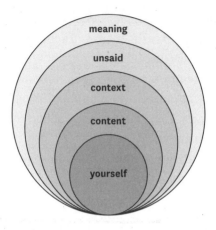

If you are looking for a recommendation on how to use this book, try reading and practicing one chapter per week, rather than reading the book from cover to cover. The power is in reflection and practice.

This book is designed to be read and to be practiced. Listening is a contact sport. When you apply and integrate these concepts into your workplace conversations, you will notice a sustained change. Listening requires practice with others if you want to make progress. At the end of each chapter, there is space for you to reflect on what you have read and to practice three simple techniques in your conversations that week.

I am reminded of my conversation with James Clear, author of the best-selling *Atomic Habits*: "You don't rise to the level of your goals; you fall to the level of your systems."[2] These reflections will become routines, rituals, and ultimately a system of practice that will support you in improving your listening in the moment of every meeting.

The aim is not to be a perfect listener, but to improve on your last discussion, so experiment as you apply these techniques into your everyday life.

Because listening is a contact sport, I recommend inviting a trusted work colleague into your practice to help you hone these techniques. There are examples of how to do this at the end of each chapter.

You are building a lifetime skill; some patience and practice will create sustainable foundations and change the way you communicate for the rest of your life.

Listening is the willingness to have your mind changed. Are you open to exploring?

Oscar

chapter 1

why listen?

---

*Listening is the willingness to
have your mind changed.*

LI WENLIANG IS an eye doctor—an ophthalmologist. Through a decade of work and study, he has built a professional reputation of care and diligence in his work and among his patients. Dr. Li is a husband and a father to a five-year-old. He and his wife are expecting their next child in a few months. When not working, he enjoys eating fried chicken and playing basketball. Since university, he has maintained close contact with a circle of academic colleagues.

On December 30, 2019, at 5:43 p.m., Dr. Li has just finished reading a disturbing report from Dr. Ai, director of emergency at Central Hospital of Wuhan, where he works. A SARS-like influenza strain that is resistant to existing treatment protocols is emerging in the hospital.

He decides to send a private message via WeChat to his university medical alumni group:

7 confirmed cases of SARS were reported from Huanan Seafood Market.

He attaches a few medical images to his post. About an hour later, he adds to his message:

The exact virus strain is being subtyped.

Remind your family members and loved ones to be on the alert.

A screenshot of his post makes its way from the private group to the broader internet. On January 3, 2020, the local police commence an investigation, and following his interview, he receives a formal reprimand for spreading false information:

We now warn and admonish you about the violation of the law that you committed when you published untrue information on the internet. Your behaviour is out of compliance with what the law allows and violates the rules of the Public Security Management Regulations of P.R. China.

It is illegal conduct.

The Public Security Department hopes that you actively cooperate, follow the advice of the People's police, and stop your illegal behavior.

Can you do it?

Answer: [Yes, I] can.

We hope that you will calm down and think carefully. We also solemnly tell you: if you are stubborn so as not to express remorse instead of continuing to carry out illegal behaviour, you will be punished by the law.

Do you understand this clearly?

Answer: [Yes, I] understand clearly.[1]

Dr. Li signs in black ink, then places his finger in red ink and presses his fingerprint on the reprimand three times, matching his signature and where he answered—*Yes, I understand clearly.*

On January 10, 2020, Dr. Li develops a cough; unbeknown to him, he has now contracted the SARS-like influenza while treating his patients. He becomes a patient in his hospital.

The virus that Dr. Li has contracted becomes known as severe acute respiratory syndrome coronavirus 2 (SARS-CoV-2), which causes COVID-19. He fights for his life, a battle that he, unfortunately, loses at 2:58 a.m. on Friday, February 7, 2020.

Before you judge the authorities in Wuhan for ignoring opinions, perspectives, and facts that they could not see, hear, understand, or disagree with, notice whether you tend to listen for what's similar or what's different. The Wuhan authorities listened exclusively for the familiar—what made immediate sense based on past patterns, education, and understanding.

Listening is the willingness to have your mind changed. Ask yourself what you would have done in this situation. Would you have focused on the similar and comfortable, or would you have been open to exploring different opinions, data, insights, perspectives, and possibilities?

Your daily conversations might not have these same global and historical consequences, yet your ability to deeply listen impacts your relationships and your professional reputation.

For individuals, the cost of not listening is fractured relationships with others in your organizations or at home. People's sense of isolation or disconnection grows when their manager doesn't invite, encourage, or prompt for contribution. The result is that people go through the motions, and human potential is wasted.

For companies, the cost of not listening is measured in lost customers, ignored employees, unsuccessful products and services, and unsustained profits.

For charities, not-for-profits, and for-purpose organizations, the cost is never achieving the changes they want to bring to the communities and countries they seek to serve. Government and public sector organizations who are obsessed with policy objectives that are formulated in comfortable office buildings grow detached from the daily struggles of the citizens they claim to serve. They increasingly become irrelevant institutions.

There were many opportunities to listen for COVID-19. Dr. Zhang Jixian, who worked through the 2003 SARS virus, noticed a viral variation in a diagnosis she made of an elderly couple on December 26, 2019.[2] The next day, Dr. Zhang reported the variant to the local center for disease control. The question is whether anyone else was listening.

In June 2020, the global death toll from COVID-19 was half a million, with ten million cases. In the same month, Dr. Li's widow, Fu Xuejie, gave birth to their second son.[3] By March 2022, six million people had died due to COVID-19.

The cost of not listening to a different perspective and point of view between the authorities and Dr. Li will have consequences for the history of humanity. I wonder what not being listened to is costing you.

The difference
between hearing and
listening is action

Better than you think

Commencing in 2018 and running continuously since then, the Deep Listening Research (see more details on page 261) is a range of surveys including numeric and verbatim data about listening barriers in English-speaking workplaces. The research explores a variety of listening issues, including self-assessed listening effectiveness. We asked participants to assess their listening effectiveness. We also asked them to assess the listening of others. Finally, we asked them to describe what they say gets in the way of great listening—for them and for others.

When asked how they would rate themselves as a listener compared to others in their workplace, 74.8 percent of respondents considered themselves either above or well above average. When asked to rate the listening of others, only 12.1 percent chose above or well above average.

What does this mean? It means that we each think we are much better listeners than other people are. Not just *much* better, but actually *six times* better.

The first listening barrier is a self-awareness bias—we think we are better at listening than others perceive us to be. We believe we are a better listener than the speaker does. There is no universal and shared understanding of the characteristics of how to listen effectively.

Common understanding

Unlike with math, language, or science, you didn't have a listening teacher. Math and science each had lessons to explain

The more senior
you are in an organization,
the more **your**
listening matters

the basics, yet when did you learn the principles and practices of listening? There was no subject called listening.

In math, the foundations are addition, subtraction, multiplication, and division. Learning English, you are taught about adjectives, nouns, and verbs. Chemistry has the periodic table of elements, which is consistent for all scientists, no matter which language they speak. But there is no universal framework for *how to listen*.

Let's look at some numbers that we will explore in more detail as we progress on our journey together. The numbers are 125, 400, and 900.

- *Talking speed:* 125 words per minute

- *Listening speed:* 400 words per minute

- *Thinking speed:* 900 words per minute

These numbers tell us that we think faster than we speak, and we listen way ahead of the speaker's talking speed.

You can listen four times faster than they can speak.

This creates many temptations for you as the listener, such as anticipating, judging, distraction and drifting away, problem-solving, or fixing the person—all while waiting for the speaker's words to catch up with your ability to process them.

For the speaker, the gap is much worse—they can think *nine times faster* than they can speak. There may be 900 words per minute in their mind, but when funneled through their tongue and mouth, they are restricted to 125 words per minute.

Within a sixty-second period, a speaker can only express 14 percent of what they may be thinking. For the listener, they are guessing and gambling about what the speaker is thinking and meaning if they only listen to the first thing that the speaker says and only engage with a narrow perspective.

The mathematics of listening and these different processing speeds are the building blocks you need to understand how to expand your knowledge of listening. After reading this book, you will listen in a lighter and more focused way.

Listening is hard

As you move across and up an organization, your listening changes, and its consequences increase. Listening moves from individual discussions to meetings with more participants: clients, employees, a board. You start to hear more complaints from inside and outside. Your listening becomes multi-dimensional. More of your attention is required—the consequences of not listening increase with your seniority. The more senior you are in an organization, the more your listening matters.

According to the International Listening Association, you spend a minimum of 50 percent of your workday listening.[4] Yet I am curious if you have allocated 50 percent of your professional development time to improving your listening skills. Adding listening to your communications toolkit will save you time and create a lifelong skill that will change your relationships at work. Everyone can benefit from spending a few more minutes each week improving their listening.

Paradoxically, conversations and meetings will be shorter and more meaningful when you increase your listening effectiveness. But that doesn't mean this will be an easy journey. Anything truly transformational rarely is.

We each think we are much better listeners than other people are. Not just *much* better, **but actually** *six times* **better.**

People say to me, "Oscar, listening is hard, and it takes too long. Why bother?" I say, "Listening is light, easy, and straightforward when you know how. Would you be open to a different approach?"

When you are open to improving your listening, conversations and projects take less time because there is less wasted effort re-explaining. The additional people, resources, and quality costs are minimized because your initial conversations are focused and more effective.

Imagine a future where your conversations, meetings, or workshops are places where no one has to repeat themselves or fight to be heard, rather than places where people are distracted or ignored or misunderstood. You have felt the cost of not listening when you have been interrupted, ignored, or spoken over, or when you have had to repeat yourself.

Mastering the art of how to listen in the modern world creates and sustains higher-quality conversations that take less effort and make a more significant impact.

The principles of listening are simple, yet the consistent daily practice takes effort. The effort is worth it. When you read this book, you will develop a powerful skill that will contribute to better relationships, faster learning, and a more significant impact on your career and community.

You might be at the stage where you are thinking, "I'm a good listener, so how do I teach my kids, co-workers, or life partner how to be a better listener?"

Be careful, because you are already teaching them "how to listen" by your own listening behavior. You are teaching through example. Listening can be taught, yet the most

powerful way to help others improve their listening is to create a great listening experience through your role modeling.

If you are a parent, you realize that your children listen more to your actions than to your words. Rather than
shouting at your children—"Why aren't you listening to
me?"—consider the listening example you are role modeling
for those children. *Are you listening to them?* Your responsibility is to be a great listening role model.

When you are in the presence of a great listener, they not
only make you feel different, they also create an experience
that changes you permanently. Let's begin becoming that listener. Here and at the end of each chapter, I will invite you
to practice three things during a discussion over the course
of the following week.

Remember, the aim is not to become a perfect listener: it's
to improve on your last conversation.

how to listen this week

1 Who is the best listener you have ever seen? What is one thing they did well?

2 When was the last time someone fully and deeply listened to you? What did they do well during that conversation?

3 When you think of that conversation, how did you think, speak, and feel differently as a result?

P.S. Earlier, I advised finding a workplace listening colleague or buddy—someone you know well and trust. They will remind, encourage, and stretch the way you practice your listening each week. Thousands of examples from our research show that listeners who find a listening buddy at work will improve, maintain, and sustain their listening better than those who treat listening as a solo pursuit. If you buy them a copy of this book, you can help each other accelerate the listening in your workplace together.

chapter 2

get ready to listen

*Listening starts before
the conversation commences.*

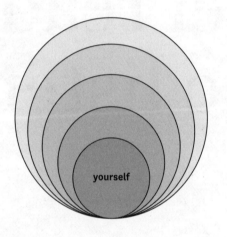

yourself

I T'S A BEAUTIFUL autumn day, and Tina, a busy working mom, is in her car on the way to pick up her three-year-old daughter from daycare. It's a twenty-five-minute drive from Tina's work to the daycare center, and Tina is finalizing a work call with Fatima while driving.

Tina had expected the call to take ten minutes. Unfortunately, the conversation is longer than expected and ends up taking the entire distance. She parks her car and continues the discussion with Fatima while she walks. When she reaches the front gate of the daycare center, she takes another ten minutes to finish the call. Eventually, she hangs up and goes through the doorway to collect her daughter.

Although Tina has disconnected the phone call, she still hasn't disconnected her mind from the issues and actions covered in the discussion—so much so that even at the door to the center she is still ruminating on Fatima's questions.

Tina's daughter is excited to see her mom; she runs and gives her a hug, bursting to tell her about her day. Her daughter launches into a wonderful story about adventures, friends, and the most specific details about castles, bridges, and rivers.

Showing her daughter how interested she is, Tina asks her lots of questions. "Who was that?" "What did you do next?" "What did you like about that?"

As Tina puts her daughter into the car seat, her daughter announces, "Mummy, why are you bumping my words?"

If her daughter was an adult, she would have said, "Stop interrupting, please!"

Tina's enthusiasm for her daughter's story is what everyone wants to experience when they are talking, right? Show interest, ask relevant questions, and pay attention. Yet her daughter experienced someone who was constantly interrupting her.

Tina's daughter wanted to tell her story—entirely, completely, and without interruption. She tried to tell the story from start to finish without questions, reactions, or solutions. Tina's questions created a disjointed conversation.

Perhaps you've had this experience, on either side of the conversation. Many people think that listening is about questioning. When your mind is absent or wandering, these questions appear random to the speaker rather than something that expands the conversation.

Aimless and arbitrary questions waste the speaker's time and diminish the relationship.

Tina thought she was listening. As they drive off, her mind divides very quickly as more issues from Fatima's call come to mind. The monkey in her mind is swinging from branch to branch, between the present, past, and future.

Her discussion with her daughter is interrupted by the phone ringing—it is Fatima again, and Tina has a decision to make about whether to answer the call or focus on her daughter.

Whether it's a phone call or our next meeting, our divided attention is one of the first barriers to listening. No matter how strongly you intend to bring your attention and focus to a conversation, listening commences before you arrive at the discussion.

Prepare by "tuning"

When a professional orchestra prepares for their performance, they tune their instruments every time, whether they are playing in the same concert hall, a new location, with regular performers, or with guests. The process and practice of tuning their instruments before they begin is crucial to creating a predictable and consistently high-quality performance.

Although a musician may have performed in the same building only twenty-four hours earlier with the identical instrument, they still humble themselves to their conductor, the audience, and fellow performers, and tune their instruments every single time. While undertaking that tuning, they are simultaneously tuning into the sound of the other instruments and performers. Tuning is a skill, a practice, and a strategy. Tuning is a sign of discipline, self-respect, and mutual respect.

Getting ready for a performance is about their physical presence—where they sit, how they sit, lighting, the placement of sheet music, and clear eye contact with the conductor.

Even if the orchestra has done it thousands of times, the practice of tuning is always an act of curiosity and care. It is a process of practice with a mindset toward mastery. When tuning, they are not going through the motions. It is

Listening is
a state of mind

deliberate, sequenced, and thorough. It is not something they can fake. You either are tuning the instrument, or you are not. This is a commitment to consistent improvement and creating a memorable experience rather than just playing music.

Professional performers will take from five to ten minutes during the tuning process. This varies based on the age of the instrument, their knowledge of the venue, and their familiarity with the music. When tuning, the orchestra is always tuning to the note A (usually 440 hertz, or vibrations per second), led either by the oboe or the first violin.

When you attend a concert or a performance, you prepare yourself to listen by taking the time to become present to the location, your physical and social surroundings. Knowing that you will be listening respectfully to the performers and the audience, you switch your mobile devices to a setting that reduces or removes distractions.

In the Deep Listening Research, switching electronic devices to silent before a discussion commenced made the most significant listening improvement for 86 percent of participants. This action makes a vast difference to your listening. Although it is easy to do, it is hard to practice.

The stories, static, and unhelpful frequencies playing in your mind before you arrive in a conversation make listening hard. Listening is demanding and draining when you compete with the chatter in your mind.

If you are in a profession or a situation where you can't switch your phone to silent, vibrate, or off, announce to the others at the beginning of the conversation that you are on-call or you are expecting a call. Explaining this before you start signals to the others that you will need to attend to

Allowing the subconscious
time to process makes
listening light and liberating
rather than draining

any call or message that arrives, and helps them understand and empathize with your circumstances. Listening *is* a state of mind.

Listening to yourself

Over twenty thousand people have completed this workshop exercise I'm about to invite you to explore. Participants have reflected on this exercise as the most potent part of the workshop.

Are you ready? I invite you to pause and move to a quiet location where you cannot be interrupted for three minutes. That's how long it will take to complete this exercise.

Read instructions 1 to 5 completely before you commence.

1 For the next three minutes, focus your eyes on a blank space, a wall, some paper—not a screen. If you can close your eyes during this exercise, even better.

2 Notice your breathing: is it slow, fast, light, or heavy?

3 Bring your attention to yourself and ask yourself this question: *What am I not listening to in myself?*

4 Switch your phone to "do not disturb" and set your alarm for three minutes.

5 Sit and ask yourself: "What am I not listening to in myself?" Do this for three minutes.

6 Please commence now.

Welcome back.

1   Did three minutes feel fast or slow?

2   Did you get distracted?

3   What did you notice?

You may notice that many random thoughts popped into your mind. Some have been percolating for a while. Some of these thoughts were part of a thinking pattern, and some new ideas may have emerged during the three minutes.

Like popcorn popping around in a pot, your thoughts may have been bouncing off other thoughts in your mind. Some are things you need to do immediately, and some have been buried for a long time and are only surfacing now.

This exercise is *not* a mindfulness meditation; it's designed to surface all of the thoughts that your subconscious is processing before you listen to someone else. Each of these thoughts will impact how you tune in and listen to yourself before starting a conversation. You start to hear what's not in tune for you very quickly.

All of the things you have been listening to during this exercise are the submerged thoughts your mind is processing before it's ready to listen to someone else. For the last three minutes, you've had a chance to listen below the surface—to listen to your subconscious thoughts and feelings.

When we are not conscious of the thoughts that our mind processes before we start a conversation, the discussion will be disjointed and out of tune. When orchestral musicians take time before every performance to prepare and tune, they create consistent and predictable results—individually and as a group. The same is true when it comes to listening.

Taking three minutes to prepare, paradoxically, will shorten discussions because you won't be distracted by subconscious thoughts, feelings, or the need to fix, interrupt, or drift away. When you are ready to listen, this creates a space for you and them.

If the conversation matters and has consequences, commit to tuning and preparing before each conversation.

Beneath the surface

When we listen to ourselves, we quickly notice what is going on beneath the surface. This part of our mind is always on, processing and negotiating the tension between immediate, critical, and long-term issues.

Allowing the subconscious time to process makes listening light and liberating rather than draining.

You might be thinking about projects, tasks on the weekend, or things related to the person you are speaking with or to other relationships. It creates an untuned conversation when your mind is thinking about all of these submerged issues. The conversation is out of sync. The timing of each contribution sounds like a clang rather than a clear note, and the result is something that is disjointed, lacks harmony, and drains the participants' energy.

Listening starts first by listening to yourself. When you take three minutes before the conversation, it shows respect to yourself and to others. It rapidly brings to the surface any potential distractions. These distractions take two forms: internal and external.

Internal distractions

Your thoughts about the person or issue you are about to discuss may spark internal distractions. It can be long-term issues you are grappling with, or a memory created by a pattern of thinking based on similar conversations. Anything can provoke an internal distraction. *(You are even distracted by reading this!)*

The crucial part of internal distractions is knowing that they will emerge at any time. During my media interviews, presentations, or workshops, people often ask me, "Oscar, how can I stop these distractions?" This may be disappointing for you, but you cannot stop distractions.

The question that I sense people are actually asking me is this: "Oscar, how do I notice distractions and adjust accordingly?"

When you take the time to tune before the conversation, you notice the distractions sooner. When you do notice the distractions sooner, don't judge yourself harshly. The process of preparing and tuning means that you observe the distraction sooner; it also means that you reengage in the discussion faster rather than drifting away longer.

There are different categories of internal distractions. These include:

- Time-based distractions, for example, the past, the present, and the future

- Anticipating distractions about the conversation, relationship, issues, and outcomes

- Connecting thoughts acting like popcorn in a pot as multiple thoughts collide and ricochet off each other

Anticipating these distractions will reduce their impact. Take, for example, a military sniper. This is a silent and focused profession. Although they may act alone in the moment, they need to consider what support they require from maps, weapons, advanced scouting intelligence, the physical land-scape, the environment, the temperature, the time of day, and the wind. They need focus, patience, discipline, and split-second timing.

Christina Bengtsson, a Swede and a former military offi-cer, is a world-champion sniper. When I spoke with her, we discussed preparing for inevitable distractions in her profes-sion. She explained:

I speak about seconds, perhaps thirty seconds. It was one shot and I need to hit a ten to win the world title. And, of course, my mind is full of all these nervous thoughts, especially thoughts connected to the future, thoughts like: "What happens if I shoot a nine, a seven? Or what if I miss the target?"

Time is ticking and the stress is very, very strong and my heartbeat very, very fast. But then, in that situation, and with practice, I knew that I was not afraid of taking two sec-onds extra. It's too nervous. [There are] thoughts like, "Why have I put myself in this terrible situation?" "No, I'm not good enough. I haven't practiced enough." "Who do you think you are that you can actually win the world champion title?"

A situation like that can feel extremely short or extremely long. And if I use that opportunity, try to get rid of the dis-tracting thoughts, and actually learn to love that moment, the time kind of feels longer than it actually is.

I took a break and I looked at a little autumn leaf that was moving a little in the wind, and I gave this little leaf just a second or two of my full attention. And in this little second, I was back to focus. I was back to a kind of silence, a situation in which it was only me, my weapon, and the targets, and no disturbing thoughts at all.[1]

Bengtsson explaining her inner monologue in microscopic detail can remind you that distraction is a common struggle. Inner monologue can't be stopped, but it can be tamed. Ironically, in light of the need to focus, Bengtsson reset her attention with an autumn leaf. While you may not have an autumn leaf in your meeting room or video conference, you do have the opportunity to notice your heartbeat, as Bengtsson did. If you can't notice your heartbeat, notice your breathing. It's a reliable proxy for your heart rate. (More on catching your breath soon.)

Internal distractions are inevitable. Rather than reacting, create a reset strategy to return your attention to the present. It could be as simple as a leaf, a pen, or the color of the speaker's eyes.

External distractions

Your environment, electronics, and other people continuously create external distractions. Some of these distractions you can anticipate, and some will be unexpected. One thing is certain: there will be distractions. External distractions could be noise, notifications—something you hear in the conversation itself could even be your biggest external distraction of all.

One thing is certain: **there will be distractions**

Planning and being conscious of external distractions allows you to anticipate them. You cannot always choose a quiet space—whether that's face-to-face or online—yet you can pick the location with the least noise inside this space. This you can control.

When it comes to online meetings, the device you are using could become a distraction. You can anticipate this and adjust accordingly.

Consider the environment, the electronics, and everyone else as three sources of potential distractions.

	ANTICIPATED	UNEXPECTED
Environment	Noise in the room Noise outside the room	Opening door Fire alarm
Electronic	Phone Computer Watch Chat TV	Online software fails
Everyone else	Their volume Their speed Their language patterns	Unexpected visitor Late visitor

When you anticipate external distractions, their impact is minimized. It becomes limited, because you can predict how to respond. The amount of time you will be distracted, consequently, will be reduced.

Heather Morris, author of the global best-seller *The Tattooist of Auschwitz*, removed all external distractions while interviewing Holocaust survivors for her book.[2] Morris focused on only listening during these discussions. She made no recording, electronic or written, while in the survivors' presence. She chose to be fully present to witness their stories. This displayed great discipline, as well as respect for the survivors. Their stories are potent because Morris was not distracted by checking the recordings or pausing any devices—she was just listening in the moment.

In the moment, she could listen to what they said and how they said it: the words, the emotion, and what it means decades later.

It's not just your ears that are a powerful listening instrument; it's your entire body. Listening is about what you hear, see, and sense. Listen from all parts of your body, including your heart, lungs, and broader nervous system. These additional listening layers help reduce the effort in comparison to when you listen exclusively with your mind. When you start to listen with your entire body, the conversation becomes lighter, simpler, and relaxed for you and the speaker.

Your ego is not your amigo

The practice of preparing to listen is the process of pausing, becoming present, and regulating the role of your ego.

Drifting while listening or fighting the urge to interrupt is a function of your ego. It's essential to notice your ego's location and direction, especially how it might hijack the conversation.

It is crucial that you notice when your ego can be productive and unproductive. Many people think the ego is a bad thing. This is not true. Your ego plays a vital role in defending and protecting you and your agenda. When your ego goes unrestrained, that is when it becomes unproductive. Rather than creating a shared understanding, an exclusive focus on your ego will seize and misdirect the conversation.

As part of the Deep Listening Research, we asked respondents to rate the top three barriers. They named attention, comprehension, and empathy. Your ego and empathy are two sides of the same coin. Your presence in a discussion can be overwhelmed by an uninhibited ego. Noticing your ego's role in a conversation will help you increase your empathy. With your ego adjusted and your empathy present, the speaker relaxes and changes how they communicate. The result is that they explain more about their thoughts and feelings.

The deeper you breathe, the deeper you listen

A conscious focus on your breath can act as a handbrake for a needy ego. Neuroscientist Romie Mushtaq recommends three minutes of controlled breathing before a conversation and a group meeting:

And what does that mindful minute of controlled breathing help us to do? We actually come to a place of calm consciousness. Taking that three minutes of controlled breathing has been scientifically shown to start to shift the stress response in the brain.

The centers of the brain known as the amygdala and hippocampus, which are processing all the incoming information, memory, and your mood, calm down. We have control of our emotions, and we have control over our thought processes. And it's that three minutes of pause that brings everybody in the room to an even playing field.[3]

You breathe 25,000 times a day, and, for the most part, you do it without thinking. Bringing awareness to your breath will improve your listening.

When I listened to James Nestor, author of *Deep: Freediving, Renegade Science, and What the Ocean Tells Us about Ourselves* and *Breath: The New Science of a Lost Art*, he explained,

Breathing is this wonderful anchor; this way of quickly listening to your body so that you can be a conduit to other knowledge out there in the world. I don't see a huge disconnect between listening and breathing because you are very closely tuning in to exactly how you're feeling.[4]

The foundational importance of breathing across all human pursuits is not a modern invention; ancient traditions across all continents describe the centrality of breathing to being effective. There are seven books in the Chinese Tao dedicated to breathing. Nestor explained:

Any breath inhaled through the mouth is considered adverse breath. Never inhale through the mouth. The benefits of the nose are that it heats up air to our body temperature, humidifies it, and removes pathogens—releasing nitric oxide, which is this fantastic molecule that can fight off things like bacteria and viruses.

Nestor provided ~~three tips for taking control of your breath~~:

1   ~~Breathe slowly.~~

2   ~~Breathe through the nose.~~

3   ~~Breathe less than you think you need~~ to.

He mentioned that the Navy Seals use ~~box breathing~~ to achieve focus before and during their missions. This is a breathing technique also used by Olympic athletes, opera singers, and world-champion snipers. I strongly recommend trying it before your next discussion.

To use this technique, ~~inhale to a count of four, hold for a count of four, exhale for a count of four, and hold for a count of four.~~

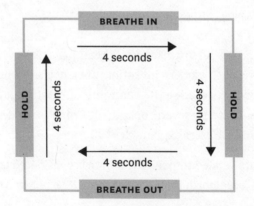

According to Nestor,

When we breathe in, that's associated with a sympathetic nervous response, which is the fight or flight response. We want balance between sympathetic and parasympathetic. When we breathe out, that's stimulating a parasympathetic response, which is the rest and relax response.

Noticing your breath before you start is essential; it is important that you notice your breath during the conversation. Use your breath to reset your focus when you are distracted. Taking a deliberate breath or doing some box breathing will reset the sympathetic and parasympathetic nervous system responses and allow your body and mind to reset and focus your attention.

At the center of Silicon Valley

In 2015, Google created a process: when a meeting had six or more people scheduled to attend, it began with a very short pause. Attendees were invited to switch off their devices and notice where their attention was and where they wanted their attention to be during the meeting.

Later that year, Google's annual employee survey, called the Googlegeist, reported that this process was one of the most referenced and productive initiatives mentioned by employees. The pause created opportunities to listen for a broader range of voices and opinions. Consequently, it generated a wider range of possible solutions. The people present in those meetings felt that the leaders listened to what they said, and other employees were more present when listening to each other.

I work with a lot of technology organizations. Usually, the only time that participants' breathing changes in group meetings is when they are reacting or responding via email or instant message on their devices with someone outside the room. Their attention is fragmented. When I draw their focus to their lack of attention to each other, keyboards fall silent, spines become upright, eye contact increases, and conversations re-commence.

Unfortunately, listening is difficult to sustain within these environments without leadership and agreed communications protocols. Thankfully, you can choose to make a change in how you show up in these meetings: by first listening to yourself. You can arrive at the meeting room early and have a deliberate pause. If you think that would look or feel awkward, try pausing in the hallway or washroom on your way to the meeting room.

If you're dialing into a virtual call, join the meeting a few minutes early and resist the impulse to send just a few more emails; instead, reflect on your purpose in that meeting. I recommend that anyone hosting a meeting commence at five minutes after the hour or half hour. That allows everyone to gather their attention and presence, and to arrive at the meeting relaxed and ready rather than rushed and distracted.

In this way, you can use the technology, instead of letting the technology use you.

If you want to go beyond the pause before a meeting, master the setting on each of your devices that controls all notifications, and use it to mute them all for the duration of

Use the technology, instead of **letting the technology use you** the meeting. It's easy to discover and activate this functionality in the software. Pressing one button to deactivate your notifications is powerfully simple to do, yet challenging to practice and sustain.

Without electronic distractions, you can focus on what the speaker says and how they say it.

As you read this, do you notice thoughts and ideas jumping like a monkey in your mind, from branch to branch and tree to tree? I wonder if technology notifications are seducing your focus while reading right now. Use the technology, don't let the technology use you.

By mastering technology, you build the foundation to listen in the moment, and to listen much longer than you imagined without interruption. Your listening becomes lighter and easier to sustain. You won't feel the urge to interrupt or drift away. When you relax and just listen, you hear with more clarity and precision, for you and for them.

It feels noticeably different for the speakers and others in the discussion. Paradoxically, the more present you are when you arrive at a conversation, the more significant your impact on the speaker. The speaker does not feel rushed, because they sense your presence. They sense your empathy rather than your impatience, judgment, or the urge to fix it or them. The speaker can be more explicit in their communications. They can take their time to explain their issue fully.

Listening is about being present and open to many possibilities. This is only possible when you build the foundation for listening and listening to yourself.

how to listen this week

1 Choose a trusted work colleague to practice with. Ask them to notice and offer feedback about how you listen in discussions with them. Invite them to observe your listening when present in group meetings with you.

2 Before each conversation, create, integrate, and practice a ritual that will help you tune your listening, just like the orchestra. It should take two to five minutes. It could be closing your eyes, taking some deep breaths, playing a song, or switching off your digital notifications. Please keep it simple and be consistent.

3 Who is the best listener you know at work? When you are in group meetings with them, become a listening detective and keep a journal of what you notice they do well as a listener. Don't try to emulate it; just observe it in action.

P.S. When I am tuning my listening, my favorite ritual is to play some music that matches the energy of the people I am about to meet with. Often it is something like "Easy" by Groove Armada, "Weightless" by Marconi Union, or "Remember the Name" by Fort Minor—each has its own unique tempo.

chapter 3

give
and pay
attention

What barriers get in the way of listening?

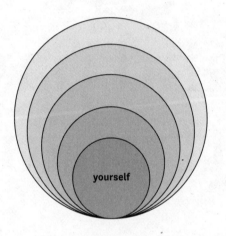

GROWING UP, AUSTRIAN-AMERICAN actress Hedy Lamarr listens to her father explaining how things work, from streetcars to printing presses. It fuels her curiosity and passion for problem-solving. At her young age, Lamarr is equally fascinated by movies and theater.

At nineteen, she marries Friedrich Mandl, chair of Austrian arms manufacturer Hirtenberger Patronen-Fabrik. She and Mandl regularly host dinner parties with influential Austrian and German defense personnel. In the privacy of their home, many top military secrets and technologies are openly discussed.

During these parties, Lamarr listens, analyzes, and learns. She develops a fascination with weapon design. Her husband and the military officials never pay her much, if any, attention. They only notice how she looks.

Mandl occasionally asks Lamarr for advice, and she gives a great deal of thought and consideration to each question. He only *hears* what she says and never acts on her recommendations—he isn't listening. As a result, Lamarr grows increasingly frustrated and disillusioned with her relationship.

Consider the backstory, too: Lamarr was born in 1914 as Hedwig (Hedy) Eva Maria Kiesler and was the only child of her Ukrainian Jewish father and Hungarian Jewish mother. The secret dinner party discussions she witnesses help her realize that war is rapidly approaching Europe. In 1937, she flees Austria and her marriage, moving to the United States.

On her journey to America, Louis B. Mayer of MGM Studios discovers her. He promotes her as the world's most beautiful woman. The phrase infuriates Lamarr because it leads to people focusing on her looks. In one interview she says, "Any girl can be glamorous. All you have to do is stand still and look stupid."

While she is building her acting career, Lamarr moves from fascinated to obsessed about weapons design to help her adopted country fight Hitler. She is motivated by the plight of her fellow Jews. Rather than follow the Hollywood party circuit, Lamarr spends all of her spare time inventing mechanical and electrical devices. A corner of her drawing room is her workshop. This helps her move her ideas from her imagination to reality.

Allied navies are suffering massive losses from German submarines, so Lamarr and her inventor-musician friend George Antheil develop a machine and file for a patent for "frequency hopping." This is a method of transmitting radio messages by rapidly changing frequencies across the signal. This technique can be used to avoid enemy eavesdropping and provide secure communications.

The U.S. Navy does not see itself relying on a patent created by an actress and a musician. They suggest that, as an actress, Lamarr could help most with the war effort by inspiring troop morale on the movie screen.

Lamarr is agitated by the fact that, yet again, she has been *ignored*. She donates the patent to the U.S. Navy to contribute to the war effort. Filed in August 1942, U.S. Patent 2.292.387 contains the foundational technology that would become integrated into sonar buoys dropped from aircraft to track submarines, and, eventually, into wi-fi and Bluetooth technologies.

Imagine what Hedy Lamarr could have invented if people had taken the time to fully listen to her ideas.

The same, yet different

The Jackson Hole Economic Symposium is an annual conference for the global finance industry. Hosted by the Federal Reserve of Kansas City, the event takes place near Yellowstone National Park. It was initially selected as a venue because the then-chair of the U.S. Federal Reserve, Paul Volcker, loved fishing for trout. This was the best way to lure him to the mountains, rivers, and lakes of Wyoming.

It's August 2005, and the industry is coming together to celebrate Alan Greenspan and his decade-long contribution to the prosperity of the U.S. and global economy as chair of the U.S. Federal Reserve. The symposium is taking place during a period of unprecedented economic growth, and the industry is gathering to present, debate, and dissect the future of global finance and trade. In the room is a who's-who of finance from Europe, China, Japan, and the United Kingdom, along with their policymakers and the bankers who lubricate global commerce.

It's probably not the place you would expect an Indian electrical engineer to be presenting a paper. Raghuram Rajan has traveled an unusual path to be in a room full of central bankers. He loves engineering, as well as J.R.R. Tolkien and *The Lord of the Rings*. Hardly the qualifications and ingredients to be one of the only two people to predict the global financial crisis of 2008.

On the Saturday morning of the conference, he gives his presentation, titled "Has Financial Development Made the World Riskier?"[1] He explains,

We were living in well-run houses where the plumbing was not a problem. And the reality was the plumbing was actually getting corroded by poor incentives in that system, and we didn't realize it until it backed up in a really big way and we asked, "What is that smell?"[2]

Despite his thorough research, methodology, and analysis, the room laughs at Rajan's unlikely conclusions. The banking experts cannot listen past their finance education, commercial incentives, and groupthink.

At the same time, on the west coast of the United States, Michael Burry is reaching similar conclusions using a very different methodology. Burry trained as a medical doctor, with a focus on neurology. Once again, not the classic pathway to be the other person to predict this global financial crisis.

Burry has been reading the detailed documentation generated through offer documents, prospectuses, and banking regulators' complex filings—those very thick documents we assume someone else has read from start to finish, and which we either delete or file away in a bankers box under the stairs. But, unlike the rest of the banking industry, Burry is reading

How well do you
notice whether you **listen**
for similarities or for
differences?

the documents from cover to cover—and is horrified by what he discovers.

Burry focuses on the microscopic details in an industry renowned for the big picture. He presents this information to the largest Wall Street banks. They also admonish, laugh at, and rebuke his findings.

The consequences of not listening to different points of view are enormous for the finance industry, for household savings, and for people's jobs globally. Millions of livelihoods and billions of dollars in savings and pensions evaporate overnight.

Burry and Rajan had a different perspective from the traditionally trained and dogmatic bankers and economists. The bankers and economists either didn't understand what they heard or chose not to listen.

Before you judge the secretary of the U.S. Treasury, the heads of the European Central Bank and the Bank of Japan, and many of the other leaders in global finance, ask yourself this: How well do you notice whether you listen for similarities or for differences?

Discovering the difference

You default to listening for similarities because your mind is a pattern-matching machine. It's anticipating and comparing what the speaker is saying at lightning speed because you can listen four times faster than they can speak. It takes great awareness to notice where your listening attention is focused—on what's familiar or dissimilar.

You have a built-in bias for noticing what's similar—to your experiences, beliefs, and knowledge. Listening to the familiar is common. I invite you to explore when this approach may be unproductive. There is another way to listen.

World-class educator John Corrigan explains that noticing the location of your attention is an essential self-awareness mindset. He contrasts childhood learning influences and how they impact your adult listening perspectives.

Corrigan says,

When we seek the familiar, we are forever comparing what we're seeing against what we already know. We're making calls on memory, and when we pull up memory, our brain actually sends a signal to the ear to suppress what the ear is hearing. One of the downsides of listening in that way is that we don't connect well to the other person.[3]

He explains that there is a relationship between listening and working memory. This is a finite resource located in the most modern part of the brain, and it is where the brain processes human communication and listening.

It's ironic that when seeking the familiar to form a connection with the speaker—a common listening barrier—we send a signal to our mind that does the opposite. The act of accessing our memory to match similar experiences takes away from working memory while attempting to allocate working memory to the function of listening. It's happening so fast that you are not conscious of how your mind is processing the multiple simultaneous activities. Corrigan says,

When seeking difference, you need to let everything in—you need to be very open in processing what they are saying rather than the sifting and sorting that takes place when listening for the familiar.

This mode assists you in exploring rather than discovering. Exploring implies no specific destination or location; discovering suggests something pre-defined to assess or locate.

Corrigan adds that modern education systems train students to a default mode of listening for the familiar. It isn't natural for adults to listen for the difference.

Notice that you have two orientations: similar and different. Neither is correct—be flexible enough in your listening to notice which one is the most productive for the discussion or decision you need to make. It's about being conscious of whether you are listening for similarities or for differences.

Listening *only* for similarities and listening *only* for differences is unsustainable and very draining for you. It narrows your attention into a dark alley with few options.

When you become aware of your default listening pattern— similar or different—choose which is productive and helpful for you and for the speaker. Be flexible; you may need to explore both approaches at different times of the discussion.

When you open your perspective, you can notice when you are listening for similarities to confirm your point of view and to help defend your position. Alternatively, when you listen for difference, are you merely creating the start of your argument because your experience, education, or evidence is different?

With this knowledge of listening for similarities or differences, be choiceful and ask which listening orientation will help you, the speaker, and the conversation. Rather than being stuck in a default orientation, and adapt to the situation. The result is more possibilities in the conversation, rather than fewer.

Listening for similarities
in an unproductive way
shows up most when you are
listening with sympathy
rather than with empathy

The power of possibility

Listening for similarities is most obvious when you notice groupthink. In seeking acceptance by the working group, people will speak and listen about a topic that reinforces the central idea or agenda. The conversation stays within safe and known boundaries or parameters when groupthink is present. Seeking to gain favor with the leader or host, the group will look for things to agree with rather than ways to explore differences.

Modern political organizations are a showcase of taking groupthink to its logical conclusion: *all* of our ideas and policies are right in *all* circumstances, and the opposing political party has *only* flawed ideas and policies in *all* circumstances.

In one-on-one discussions, listening for similarities in an unproductive way shows up most when you are listening with sympathy rather than with empathy.

I am struggling with my supervisor, they are absent most of the time and vague when I get to speak to them.

In listening for the familiar, your mind accesses your historical memory. Your mind recalls an example when you had something similar happen to you.

I had an even worse manager, they canceled our meetings at the last minute with no explanation, our team all had the same issue, we didn't have team meetings, it was the worst eighteen months of my working life.

The Deep Listening Research respondents describe the absence of empathy as *disrespected, ignored, judged, a problem to be fixed.*

Theresa Wiseman, a nurse tutor at the Bloomsbury and Islington College of Nursing and Midwifery, deconstructs empathy into four components in a paper published in the *Journal of Advanced Nursing*:[4]

1   See the world as others see it

2   Non-judgmental

3   Understanding another's feelings

4   Communicate the understanding

Renowned researcher Brené Brown has said, "Empathy is a way to connect to the emotion another person is experiencing; it doesn't require that we have experienced the same situation they are going through. People often confuse sympathy with empathy. Sympathy is I feel bad *for* you. Empathy is I feel *with* you."[5]

From the speaker's perspective, empathy is an important signal that you are listening. Yet when your attention is distracted and you don't comprehend what is being said, a lack of empathy is unavoidable.

Puzzle pieces

When you listen to differences, it is just as important to understand how you are listening for these differences.

If you are in a group discussing a new topic and they are in the process of exploring the issue, this is like constructing a jigsaw puzzle. Typically, people will start with the edges of the puzzle—the known or standard approach. The edges have one or two very straight lines that allow the puzzle's remaining pieces to be lined up and fit together.

Most people enter a group discussion with a consistent approach. What and where are the edges, the conditions, the assumptions? A rare group of participants explicitly considers what we are excluding from the discussion.

When listening for difference, make the implicit explicit by announcing your point of view as early as possible in the conversation. As the listener, your role is to create the conditions where the speaker will be comfortable sharing these views because you have made it safe.

If you hold a different perspective, declare it early rather than wait until the end, when your different perspective can feel like a conversational hand grenade—blowing up the progress that others believe they have made.

Equally, constantly declaring a repetitive point of difference can be unproductive for the group. Be mindful that sometimes listening for differences can derail, destabilize, and disorient the group.

When bringing consensus to a group, listening for similarities is essential. Listening for similarities is vital to define a common or standard set of values or operating principles. If you're undertaking research, whether through focus groups or one-on-one conversations in an organization listening for similarities, it's vital to establish the key themes. Organizing common themes helps you take faster actions. This is when listening for similarities is powerful and productive. Consistently exploring similarities and differences throughout the discussion is a sign of effective listening.

"Sometimes they'll be saying something, and then they'll sigh and they'll stop, and they'll give a moment of silence. **And then they'll say what they really want to say.**"

When a project begins in a working group, we need to define an expected outcome to help everyone understand their role. As the project leader, it is critical to create a shared understanding. The best way to achieve this at the beginning of the project is to ask these three questions:

1   What drew you to this project?

2   What is the purpose of this project?

3   What do you want to achieve on this project?

In this setting, the leader and the group are looking and listening for "what do I have in common." In the early stage of a project, people seek to understand commonalities through past experience. This helps the group listen for connection and purpose.

Only once the common purpose for the group has been established can the leader and the group effectively understand where they will discover their differences.

Listening for the capital letters

When listening for similarity and difference, often it's as simple as listening for emphasis. Visual scribe Anthony Weeks describes this as finding the speaker's language patterns. Weeks says:

Inflection or points of emphasis where you could visualize it being said by them with capital letters.

Listening for those capital letters is to say, "Ah, that's it.

That's what they really mean to say." Or, "That's important to them. I'm going to write that in capital letters because that sounds like it's a big deal." When they say, "So what I really mean to say is..." they're ready to say something important. Sometimes it's more subtle. They'll be saying something, and then they'll sigh and they'll stop, and they'll give a moment of silence. And then they'll say what they really want to say.[6]

When you listen for similarities, you will struggle to distinguish the capital letters and differences. When you are listening for contrast, it becomes much easier to notice when differences emerge in what they are saying and how they are saying it.

Listening to differences across genders

Now that you are conscious that you listen through your filters and biases, let's address a question I'm often asked: Do women and men listen differently?

In their 1995 study "The Listening Styles Profile," Watson, Baker, and Weaver asked 1,799 undergraduate students sixteen questions to rate their listening in four categories: people, action, content, and time-oriented styles.[7] This is what they found:

People-oriented listening emerged as a style where concern for others' feelings and emotions was paramount. People-oriented listeners tried to find areas of common interest with others and respond empathetically to them.

The *action-oriented* listening style reflected a preference for receiving concise, error-free presentations. Action-oriented listeners appeared to be particularly impatient and easily frustrated when listening to a disorganized presentation.

Content-oriented listening reflected a preference for receiving complex and challenging information. Content-oriented listeners tended to evaluate facts and details carefully before forming judgments and opinions.

The *time-oriented* listening style involved a preference for brief or hurried interactions with others. Time-oriented listeners tended to let others know how much time they had to listen or tell others how long they had to meet.

In their findings, the researchers conclude that women and men listen differently: "Females endorsed the people and content styles more strongly while males oriented more toward the action and time styles."

In the 2001 study "Temporal Lobe Activation Demonstrates Sex-Based Differences during Passive Listening," Phillips, Lowe, Lurito, Dzemidzic, and Mathews demonstrate that different parts of the brain activate when women and men listen to the same information.[8]

Jack Zenger took this study to its logical conclusion and created an assessment in which 4,306 participants rated their listening.[9] Then, unlike in other studies, he extended the evaluation to allow others to rate the listening of the person who took the initial assessment. He found that when men and women were compared, "females proved to be significantly better listeners" and "demonstrated a significantly stronger preference for listening than males." Zenger also concluded that listening ability improves with age. (Ironically, hearing ability may decrease with age.)

Getting back to whether women and men listen differently, the evidence is mixed and so too is the proposition that one gender listens "better." I recommend that, whatever your starting position, each of us can improve our listening one conversation at a time.

Implicit bias

Quilting involves using your hands in intricate maneuvers. It requires a great deal of dexterity and fine motor skills. In an interview with NPR, Harvard psychologist Mahzarin Banaji explained that her friend, Carla Kaplan, is a passionate quilter.

She was washing a big crystal bowl in her kitchen; it slipped and it cut her hand quite severely. The gash went from Kaplan's palm to her wrist.

She raced over to Yale–New Haven Hospital. Pretty much the first thing she told the ER doctor was that she was a quilter. She was worried about her hand. The doctor reassured her and started to stitch her up. He was doing a perfectly competent job, she says.

But at this moment someone spotted Kaplan. It was a student, who was a volunteer at the hospital.

The student saw her, recognized her, and said, "Professor Kaplan, what are you doing here?"

The ER doctor froze. He looked at Kaplan. He asked the bleeding young woman if she was a Yale faculty member. Kaplan told him she was.

Everything changed in an instant. The hospital tracked down the best-known hand specialist in New England. They brought in a whole team of doctors. They operated for hours and tried to save practically every last nerve.[10]

Before you judge the emergency doctor, what were you thinking about Kaplan's hand, the cut, and quilting? Was the story something that might be familiar or different to you and your experience? Bias is a barrier to our listening and our actions. Bias enables our primary listening default to notice similarities.

Banaji and fellow psychology researcher Anthony Greenwald created the Implicit Association Test, which helps to increase your awareness of the speed of your mind's hidden associations. Over twenty million people around the globe have taken the test. It is designed to increase the consciousness of your associations and consequent bias.

Ultimately, where you direct your attention can be focused on the common or the contrast, the familiar or the variation, the similar or the different—it's a function of where your attention is fixated, and it is affected by relationship and by context.

Relational

You will listen differently to a police officer than you would to a school principal—or to an actor compared to an accountant,

When you try to stop your distractions, you give those distractions power and energy. Rather than stop them, learn to dance more skillfully with them.

or your mother versus a mechanic. Your attention will show up differently depending on who you are listening to.

Whether you have a lifelong relationship or are meeting someone for the first time, you will bring a different type of attention to the preparation and the conversation. As many commented in the Deep Listening Research, the longer the relationship, the less conscious they are of their attention in the moment. And the more likely they will be to use assumptions and mental shortcuts to anticipate, jump ahead, or interrupt the speaker.

In group discussions, listening varies based not only on the length of people's relationships. It also varies based on the task or project the group is undertaking. Respondents commented that they listened differently at the beginning of a project compared to the middle of the work-in-progress.

Contextual

The context is co-created by the participants and influenced by the content of the conversation. The context of a group discussion is dramatically different from intimate individual interaction. In a group discussion, you are listening to the speaker and the other participants simultaneously. You are listening to what the speaker is saying and watching the non-speaking participants' visual signals. You are using your peripheral vision and hearing.

In a group, your listening is like a radar constantly scanning and tuning, whereas you can focus more narrowly during an individual interaction. The content drives the context of the discussion. Your attention will vary dramatically if the context is about creativity, collaboration, conflict, competition, information sharing, or decision-making.

In the Deep Listening Research, respondents noted that their attention varied whether listening to stories or statistics, drama or details, simple or complex, familiar or different. Their attention was influenced by the vocal variation of the speaker—monotone versus range.

In group discussions, the respondents' attention was influenced by what was at risk for them during the discussion. They reported that their attention was influenced by the seniority of participants and the risk of the outcome or decision they were participating in. This comment sums it up: "If it's a regular update, I'm relaxed, yet if it's a restructure—my attention is in the zone."[11]

Notice, then reset

I want you to pause and reflect. Where is your attention in this moment, while you are reading this sentence?

It's one thing to read the words above and let them wash over you. Or you might be noticing your mindset while reading. Now is a wonderful opportunity to notice the location of your attention at this moment.

Noticing and adjusting the position of your attention during a discussion is a crucial foundation stone to increasing your listening capacity.

Keynote audiences and workshop participants often ask me, "Oscar, how do I stop from being distracted?" Here's what I say: When you try to stop your distractions, you give those distractions power and energy. Rather than stop them, learn to dance more skillfully with them.

When your attention is in, you are fixated on yourself. You and your ego are waltzing, entranced in a dance in your mind. Your ego is the neediest part of your mind. It seduces your attention and captures it for extended periods of time as you dance together safely and close, in a spell not to be broken by the reality of the outside world.

When your attention is out, it's still dancing skillfully together with your ego. Your waltz continues to be intimate and seductive, yet you notice that you are on a dance floor with another. They too are dancing with their egos. When your attention is out, you can notice beyond yourself. You can see other ways to waltz and other opportunities to engage. When you notice becoming distracted, adjust the location of your attention. Like dancing, it's only one step in a slightly different direction. And the result is that you are not bumping into either the speaker or the other dancers.

Paying versus giving attention

Let's discover the difference between paying and giving attention. Paying attention feels like a form of taxation. It's a duty, obligation, or responsibility. You go through the motions because you sense it's the socially acceptable way to be in a conversation. When you pay attention, your focus is on you. You are listening from your side of the discussion.

If you are a regular traveler listening to the flight safety announcement, you pay attention. You do it because you *have* to listen. Your mindset is "there is information that needs to be said," so you go through the motions of listening. You know what they are going to say because you have heard it before. You could recite the flight safety announcement from memory.

Imagine if on that flight, at 30,000 feet, the captain comes on while you are experiencing turbulence and explains that the crew will need to go through the flight safety announcement. You rapidly move your attention from the captain to the crew, who will provide you with the information from the pre-flight safety announcement. In this moment, you are *giving* your complete and undivided attention. Nothing will get in the way of you watching and listening to the safety announcement.

As the crew explains the exits, you count the number of rows to the exit, and you make sure you look exactly where the flight crew are pointing when they show you where the closest exit is located. You fight the urge to know which is the closest exit looking forward, remembering how the flight crew said that the nearest exit could be behind you.

In this moment, your attention narrows, and its focus is precise because nothing is more important to you than understanding these safety instructions. You collect the flight safety card from your seat pocket, which you have never looked at before now. You read the safety card with your complete and undivided attention. You study the information on the safety card that locates you, your seat, and the exit.

Your attention is finite and flexible. Whether you choose to pay or give attention, it's critical to understand that it's neither right nor wrong. It's a choice about where to direct your attention in the moment and what's appropriate in the current situation, context, or relationship.

When you pay attention, you feel constrained, restricted, and limited. It makes listening feel like a task or a chore. Paying attention is most effective when dealing with well-known situations and relationships—routine matters with predictable pathways.

Giving attention is most appropriate in emerging or evolving or emergency situations. It comes from a very different place than paying attention. It is an act of curiosity, generosity, and possibilities. When you give your complete attention, you notice what they say and what they haven't said. You notice the connection between what and how they say it. This is all possible because your working memory can attend to your listening. Consequently, it is much easier to pause and be patient.

It is impossible to *give* your complete and undivided attention to 100 percent of people and conversations, 100 percent of the time. Continuously giving your attention has its downsides. Giving attention for too long can be draining and overwhelming—be careful to notice your attention before arriving in a conversation.

I'm inviting you to notice what sort of attention you bring before, during, and after a conversation. A skillful listener will choose when paying attention is effective and efficient and will adjust to give attention appropriately.

The myth of multi-tasking

Stefan van der Stigchel is a global expert on the topic of attention and how to focus it effectively. He has written *How Attention Works: Finding Your Way in a World Full of Distraction* and *Concentration: Staying Focused in Times of Distractions.* He explains that multi-tasking is possible for routine tasks like listening to music while driving the car or washing the dishes. Multi-tasking is not possible while listening to someone else.

Van der Stigchel explains that listening is a complex task that consumes working memory. Working memory is fragile, finite, and easily overwhelmed. That's why making lists, for example, can help if you're overwhelmed and trying to remember everything (tasks, groceries) in the short term.

To effectively listen—rather than just hear—you need to comprehend, remember, and contribute to the conversation. Therefore, you will be using the majority of your working memory. To effectively use working memory, you need to bring your available attention into focus and minimize distractions, including from electronic devices. Van der Stigchel explains:

Listening is very difficult because you use working memory when you listen to a conversation. Working memory can actually only perform one task at a time.

What's difficult when you listen is that the only thing you should do is listen.

Attention is the gateway into working memory. Working memory allows conscious thought—it's impossible to think about something that has not been attended.

This could be something internal or external. Therefore it's crucial to capture someone's attention if you want to convey a message, because without attention it can never reach working memory.

Once it has entered working memory, the information has to stay there. That's complicated, because for information to stay in working memory, it needs to be repeated; it needs to be actively repeated.

When we're asked to remember a complicated phone number, we need to repeat it, or else we might lose that information.

Therefore, listening is difficult because it requires working memory.

Working memory is fragile, and it's very easy for information to be lost.[12]

Working memory is a foundational and finite resource in your listening toolkit. You need to understand that, while multi-tasking is possible for mundane and repetitive tasks, listening is not a routine or predictable task. Listening requires your focus and your deliberate management of your working memory.

Your mind is waiting for the speaker—and while it's waiting, it's **anticipating what they might say next**

You're a fast listener

It's worthwhile knowing that your brain is wired for distraction when listening. When you see, you have peripheral vision. You have peripheral hearing too—you are constantly scanning your surroundings for additional noise, sound, and threats. It's possible because there is a significant difference between the speaker's speaking speed and your listening speed.

The 125/400 Rule defines the number of words per minute the speaker communicates and the number of words per minute you can listen to.

While the speaker is speaking between 125 to 150 words per minute, you can listen to 400 words per minute. There is a considerable gap in processing time, and if you don't notice where your attention is, you could easily drift off within the first twenty seconds of the conversation. Your mind is waiting for the speaker—and while it's waiting, it's anticipating what they might say next.

Your mind predicts based on your assumptions and experience about what might be said next. Your mind could be accessing your memory from the last conversation with the speaker or from a similar theme. It is even happening for you while you are reading. Your mind moves fast.

The neuroscience of working memory explains that you can listen much faster than humans can speak. The playback speed of audiobooks or podcasts can be set up to two times faster than normal. You can retain and completely comprehend while listening to these accelerated speeds if the accent and language pattern is familiar to you.

So don't worry if you're drifting or distracted, maybe even both, while listening. Sometimes this can be an essential place of rest and recharge for your working memory. Choosing to refocus can get you back on the listening track, and the speaker usually doesn't mind you asking them to repeat what they said. (Just don't do it too often.)

Listening beyond words

Whether you are in a paired discussion or a group discussion, the first step is noticing your attention. Your presence and focus during a conversation help you hear their words, sentences, and stories. With your attention present, you can start to listen beyond the words. You start to hear the emotion in their voice and their body language because your attention is dancing between you and the speaker.

Your attention will create a space for everyone to become present, including the speaker. When you are present and bringing your attention, you will change how the speaker talks and communicates their ideas. The speaker's thinking will be different, as they don't feel rushed to explain their ideas instantly. *Build a solid foundation with your attention or risk a wasted conversation.*

Paradoxically, your attention and listening will impact how the speaker brings their attention to the conversation. Bringing your attention to a discussion, you create a clear space in the speaker's mind and in yours.

Consequentially, the speaker explores more of what they think and mean when they are speaking. Communications become clear, and your listening effectiveness increases.

Drawing your attention
to the speaker

is

like

a

tuning

fork

for their mind

Uri Hasson, a professor of psychology and neuroscience at Princeton University, was part of a team that researched how the listener's brain responds when a speaker tells stories. The research, which Hasson explains in his TED talk, shows that the listener influences the speaker.[13]

Don't underestimate how important your attention is in creating a powerful impact. Through your presence, you can fully utilize the power of listening to influence everyone's ability to communicate, including your own. Holding space for the speaker will affect what you achieve from the conversation.

Being attentive happens when you bring openness and curiosity. Although it might feel slower at the beginning, the impact is delayed and magnified. When done well, listening will consistently shorten the total amount of time spent communicating. The outcomes are powerful and impactful for each party because the discussion focuses on critical issues and their meanings rather than surface-level dialogue and arguments.

Your attention forms the foundation for the success of the situation, context, relationship, and outcomes. Without this foundation, more words, sentences, and stories create increased misunderstanding, frustration, and tension in the time available for the discussion, and undermine the relationship and the outcome.

Whether you are in a paired conversation or a group discussion, the location and orientation of your attention will impact your listening quality. The Deep Listening Research respondents highlighted that what frustrates speakers the most is when listeners are distracted by devices and/or are drifting throughout the conversation. Your attention and ongoing focus will signal to the speaker that you are hearing and listening.

Your attention invites the speaker to explore their emotions and encourages them to express their feelings in a way they may never have understood or explored.

It's your presence and focus that send powerful signals to the speaker to help them tune in to their head and their heart—their thoughts and feelings. This moves the conversation from monologue to dialogue because your listening presence is drawing more out of the speaker.

When you listen while bringing your attention, the speaker explores, evaluates, and communicates ideas previously poorly expressed or buried in their mind. It is your presence and the orientation of your attention as a listener that transforms the quality of their thinking. Drawing your attention to the speaker is like a tuning fork for their mind.

You can only bring your presence to the speaker when you are present to yourself. It's impossible to listen to the speaker when you are unavailable because your attention is elsewhere.

When the speaker experiences you as distracted and fragmented, without your attention and focus, they repeat themselves and feel like the discussion is a waste of time. The Deep Listening Research respondents explained this using language including *disrespected*, *ignored*, and *judged*.

When you bring your complete attention to the conversation, the most remarkable thing happens for you. When the speaker experiences what your attention brings to the discussion, they notice it, mention it, and ultimately mirror it when they listen to you.

how to listen this week

1   When your attention strays, reset your focus by checking the color of the speaker's eyes. It's a micro-reset of two to three seconds. A word of caution: extended eye-to-eye contact isn't appropriate in all cultures.

2   Take a longer and deeper breath when your attention strays for an extended period.

3   Notice the signals from your body about your attention. When you notice you are drifting or distracted, adjust the position of your spine, neck, or body.

P.S. The difference between hearing and listening is action. How did you do with last week's actions? Did you find a listening colleague at work to join on your *How to Listen* journey?

hear, see, and sense

---

*Listen with all of your body,
rather than only with your ears.*

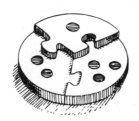

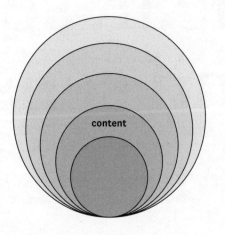

content

GROWING UP IN the countryside of northeast Scotland, Evelyn Glennie is fascinated by animals and passionate about music and dance. She begins playing the piano at the age of ten. Her father, Herbert, is her musical example as a local Methlick dance band member.

A couple of years later, while at Ellon Academy, she meets a man who radically alters the trajectory of her life. Ron Forbes is a teacher at the academy. He notices and hears what others don't: her immense potential as a musician.

Unlike other teachers, Forbes listens for subtle signals and differences. Her playing intrigues him because she plays barefoot to better connect with the vibrations and to fully feel the music in her body.

Unfortunately, she has been progressively losing her hearing—something that started in her childhood. Forbes listens beyond her deafness and senses more, choosing not to focus on the limits that others see. By the age of twelve, Glennie has become profoundly deaf.

Today, Glennie says of Forbes:

He had the discipline of the army, hard work and focus, and he also had a flexible mindset. Hearing the sounds was not going to be easy. He had to find a way.

He struck a timpani and I realized that it vibrated. He realized... there was a resonance. He asked me, "Can you feel that sound?"

That question turned my life upside down. It completely changed my life and completely changed my relationship with sound.[1]

Forbes encouraged Glennie to explore percussion rather than only one instrument. Percussionists play many instruments, including timpani, xylophone, cymbals, triangle, snare drum, bass drum, tambourine, maracas, gongs, chimes, celesta, and the piano.

Intensely focused on becoming a soloist, she moved to London by seventeen and applied to enter the Royal Academy of Music. Unlike Forbes, the administrators at the Royal Academy listened for similarities and not for differences and so struggled to understand how a deaf person could join their academy.

She was determined, and the academy provided her a second chance to share the potential and possibilities that she, her dad, and her music teacher had imagined. Eventually, she was accepted and rapidly advanced by collaborating with various musicians and musical genres.

Glennie was ahead of her time musically and professionally. Television appearances and international music venues would showcase her passionate and energetic music for many decades. At the age of twenty-eight, she received the Order of the British Empire for her contribution to music and for removing barriers for future musicians.

Like Dame Evelyn, you have a Ron Forbes in life. A teacher so curious, thoughtful, and intrigued about your potential. These teachers have a profound impact on our lives. These teachers listen beyond our words and actions and can sense the essence of what we yearn for rather than what we yell out aloud.

I wonder who your Ron Forbes is?

There is one thing I know to be true: no matter how long ago you were at school, you can instantly recall the name of that teacher who listened for your potential.

This is the impact that listening can have on others when you know how to hear, see, and sense—how to listen.

A moment of pause

Before we begin, it's important to recap where you've just been and why. The practice of deep listening means that first you must get ready to listen, to tune in to yourself so that you can make room for listening to others.

Only now can you start to adjust your focus from yourself, toward the speaker. You begin to build the layers of listening as you integrate listening to yourself while listening to the speaker. This is a new layer, where you move to listen to their words, sentences, and stories.

This adjustment in focus brings the element of dance to the process. Now there are two people. There are unforeseen moments, components that require more concentration and focus, and factors that emerge in the liminal space between you and the speaker.

What emerges in the conversation is the third component for you and the speaker: the dialogue. The dialogue has its unique elements, shape, texture, and gravity. The discussion takes on a different color for each of the participants. The speaker might be speaking in blue, and you may be listening in red. The result could be a purple discussion as the two colors combine.

When listening to the speaker's content, there are three discrete and integrated elements: hear, see, and sense.

Each element will help you build more awareness of the next layer in your listening. Approach each component in sequence—hear, see, and sense. Although you will have the capacity to do all three simultaneously, focus, practice, and progress in order.

We will explore each of these in turn:

1   *Hear:* the audio content that your ears, body, and mind capture

2   *See:* their facial expression and body language

3   *Sense:* the emotion present during the discussion

Let's start with hearing.

Hear: Listening with your body

With your presence, attention, and focus in place, hearing and comprehending what the speaker says is a vital part of their experience of being listened to. When people speak, they typically communicate in two distinct ways—stories or statistics, big picture or details, ideas or tasks.

Each speaker will have a primary speaking preference. Neither is right or wrong; it's simply their preference. Equally, you have a communication preference. It is vital that you are aware of this preference, otherwise it will become a barrier or a filter to your listening.

There could be a match in styles or a disconnect between your communication preference and the speaker's. The important thing is to notice what you are focused on when hearing. Your hearing is like a magnet. It will either be attracted to the speaker's words or repelled.

When you hear what they say, be aware and notice their primary communication style to help you hear and listen to what they are saying. To make it simple, you can break the speaker's approach down into two primary ways of communicating their content: stories or statistics.

Stories have a beginning, middle, and end. They have characters, heroes, and villains, and the speaker is either a character in or a narrator of the story. The stories have a journey, problem, tension, or struggle, and sometimes they have a resolution or an outcome and sometimes not.

Speakers with a communications preference for statistics are detailed, specific, sequential. They value accuracy over anecdotes and prefer clear actions with dates, times, owners, and actions.

Mismatched preferences between the speaker's preferred style and yours will accelerate how quickly you drift away

The following are two descriptions of the same event. The description is being given by two participants in an identical meeting, yet there are two different stories. They are different in detail, emotion, perspective, focus, and outcome.

Project Recovery: The story

Project Recovery started about four months ago, and it has been a struggle between Peta in finance and Mark from sales. Peta says we need to increase our prices, and Mark says the customers won't be happy with the price rise and they will choose the competitor with better prices.

Every week, Mark leads a meeting between the sales team, and Peta attends to get a better sense of whether price increases are a challenge for all the sellers or just for Mark. Peta sits in the weekly meeting, collecting evidence against Mark.

I'm squeezed between our customers, Mark, and Peta.

Project Recovery: The statistics version

On January 15, the sales and finance teams met to discuss Project Recovery. There were eight other people in the meeting: four from finance—Peta, Simon, Amy, and Curt; one from customer service—Casey; and three from sales—Mark, the sales leader, plus Jessica and Emma.

The agenda item was a 15.25 percent price increase and Peta from finance presented a spreadsheet with the last nine months of sales data, our pricing, the pricing of the competition, and the number of sales proposals that were negotiated.

The discussion went for twenty-five minutes, and it was a debate between Peta and Mark. No one else in the meeting made a contribution, except for Simon, who provided additional data about invoicing and payment timing.

Nothing was agreed, other than for Peta to attend the regular sales meeting to understand the feedback of the other seven sellers who weren't present in the initial meeting.

Peta arrives at the sales meetings, which happen on Mondays at 9:30 a.m. for forty-five minutes, with her notepad and laptop. Peta takes notes, occasionally updating a spreadsheet she keeps on her laptop. Simon from finance attends these sales meetings each fortnight and takes notes also.

Peta and my manager, Mark, meet once a week on a Wednesday for thirty minutes. Nothing is formally communicated to us about the outcome from these meetings.

I am not clear if or when I should include the new pricing on customer proposals. Currently, I have six proposals that are due to be submitted to customers in the next seven days.

You have just read two versions of an identical situation, each description with different communications methods. While reading each one, you will notice that one story was more engaging for you.

It's common to have a preference for one over the other. Neither is correct nor incorrect, and the important thing is to be aware of your preference and understand that you can't control the speaker's style.

Being conscious and flexible enough to notice a mismatch and reset accordingly is the skill. It may take a little longer to notice the speaker's style when you meet them for the first time.

It's essential to notice how you hear them. It provides an early warning signal to how quickly you will be distracted in the discussion. Mismatched preferences between the speaker's preferred style and yours will accelerate how quickly you drift away.

Acoustics

Acoustics are the properties of sound in the location you find yourself in during a conversation. You can't listen if your hearing is distracted by other noise. Does the agreed location have the right acoustics for the dialogue?

The building, room, ceiling height, door, machinery, production lines, and seating arrangements impact indoor acoustics. Flooring, furniture, and curtains also influence acoustics.

Whether it is the wind or the traffic that impacts you, or the speaker's position, or that of the people surrounding the conversation—walking, standing, or speaking—you can influence your ability to hear effectively.

When it comes to environmental acoustics, you have more influence and choice than you think. You can change locations, seating arrangements, or whether the discussion takes place sitting, standing, walking, or online.

Here are the primary questions you want to ask yourself and the other participants:

1 Where is the most effective location for the discussion and the outcome?

2 What can we adjust to improve the acoustics during the conversation?

3 How can I ensure I hear the speaker clearly during a group discussion?

Cam Hough is the lead violin for the Brisbane Philharmonic Orchestra. The lead violin is an intermediary between the conductor and the orchestra. One of their tasks is to lead the tuning before the performance. He explains that tuning is about harmony.

When the notes resonate with you, there is a mathematical relationship between sound frequencies. The same is true when it comes to hearing someone else. Unless you tune your hearing into their stories or statistics, you will create a dissonance that reduces your ability to hear.

Hough is also a world-class acoustic engineer. An acoustic engineer ensures that work, performance, and public spaces are tuned to enable humans to hear each other and what is being performed from the stage.

I asked Hough for his recommendation about adjusting workplace environments to improve listening. Here is what he said:

The first is: can you see them? If there's line of sight, there's usually line of sound. The second is just how quiet or loud the office itself is. The third is looking at the reflections. If there are big surfaces where someone is listening that [are] hard and reflective, they will reflect sound very easily. Sometimes it's putting things on walls—that can be soft furnishing and foam that can absorb sound—because they will take some of these reflections out of the way.[2]

Paraphrasing

Paraphrasing is the process of reflecting to the speaker what was said and heard. It is an opportunity to increase shared comprehension. Paraphrasing assists the speaker as much as the listener. When done well, effective paraphrasing confirms what was said, heard, and understood for the speaker and the listener. When done poorly, paraphrasing sounds meaningless and hollow. "Yeah," "Yes," "Right," "Of course."

Paraphrasing could take the form of a statement or reflective question. Effective paraphrasing advances the understanding of the speaker and the listener. It needs to be consistent and not repetitive, neutral and not robotic.

A word of caution: *paraphrasing is reflection, not interpretation.* When paraphrasing with your interpretation, the speaker may feel corrected, judged, or misunderstood.

Paraphrasing can be a chance to use your note-taking practice to capture key points of emphasis or something that might require clarification. Be aware of the language you use when you paraphrase.

Paraphrasing
is reflection, not
interpretation

AVOID	FOCUS
Interpreting their words	Summarize in their words
Drawing conclusions	Be curious
Only summarizing once	Be consistent
Statements	Ask
So, what you meant was...	Do you mean...?
So, what you just said was...	Are you saying...?

Neutral paraphrasing allows the speaker and the listener to confirm their shared comprehension.

See: Listening with your eyes

Listening is collecting verbal and non-verbal content. After listening to the words, you should collect as many visual signals as you can comfortably process. Your eyes are an important part of creating a connection between you and the speaker.

Eye level

Cam Hough may be an expert on the auditory environment, yet his strongest recommendation for successful listening is aligning to eye level.

Eye level is ear level and helps the speaker to be heard. Your eyes and ears are at approximately the same height on your head. We have evolved as a species to communicate with sight and sound aligned.

Unlike other primate family members, humans have white in their eyes. This helped us distinguish humans from other species and created cooperation and connection. Our eyes signal a unique link between each other and are an essential ingredient in the way humans communicate.

The Deep Listening Research reinforces that your eyes signal to the speaker the location of your attention. When your eyes are focused on a phone or a computer, the speaker believes this to be disrespectful and or distracted. When your eyes make no contact for an extended period of time, the speaker reads this as disinterest or drifting attention. Either way, your eyes are a critical part of listening.

Research released by Quantified notes that "adults make eye contact between 30 percent and 60 percent of the time in an average conversation. However, to make an emotional connection, the ideal amount of eye contact is between 60 percent and 70 percent. Direct eye contact held for more than ten seconds at a time is unnerving for the person you are talking to."[3]

A word of caution. The research from Quantified was conducted using Western workplaces and cultures. In some cultures, holding extended eye contact with the speaker, especially if they are senior in age or in the organization's hierarchy, may be perceived as a signal of disrespect. In other cultures, extended eye contact between women and men may be considered inappropriate.

Justin Coulson is a psychologist, the co-host of the parenting-advice program *Parental Guidance*, and a father to six girls, making him a parenting expert with real-world experience. Like all experts, Coulson is humble and happy to admit he doesn't always get it right. He explained to me his experience with his daughter:

When she was only three, I was in the kitchen—I'm cooking, I've got the oil in the pan, I've got the onions, I've squirted some garlic, and now I'm looking at the recipe in the cookbook.

I become aware that my little girl Abbie is sort of tugging on my pant leg and just saying, "Dad, Dad, Dad, Dad, Dad." And I'm like, "Abbie, not now. I'm busy. I'm doing important things. I'm cooking our dinner."

And I'm trying to read, and stir, and deal with her, and it occurred to me after about twenty seconds that I'm a parenting expert and my daughter wants my attention.

I can probably turn the stove off, or turn away from what I'm doing just now and pay attention to her; I can stop, look, and listen.

I stopped what I was doing, crouched in front of her, picked up her two little hands, and held them in mine.

I looked her in the eyes and said, "Abbie, I'm sorry for not listening to you properly. I know you've been trying to talk to me. I'm listening now. Would you like to tell me what it is that you want to say?"

Abbie looked at me, put her head on one side, smiled, and said, "I love you, Dad." Then she skipped off into the living room. She only needed five seconds of my time, and she just wanted to tell me that she loved me. And I almost missed that opportunity because I was so busy doing other things that I thought were more important.[4]

It's a great story about attention and listening, yet I also want to draw your attention to something Coulson did. I asked him about his choice to crouch down and connect with his daughter at eye level.

He explained that eye contact is "a human thing":

Making eye contact, especially with infants and toddlers, is absolutely vital and is associated with them feeling that sense of connection. When you make a connection with your eyes, it draws attention, it draws focus, it says, "I'm noticing you. I'm paying attention to you."

Not only did I crouch down, I also met her eyes and made sure that we were gazing at one another. It's a way that we recognize their humanity; it's the way that we demonstrate intimacy. And what happens when we both make eye contact and touch... is, neurologically, their brain starts to release a whole lot of neurotransmitters, hormones, that help them feel calm and centered—the brain releases serotonin.

Most people think that dopamine is this excitatory, stimulatory chemical, but it also is involved in the regulation of emotion and calming. The dopamine and serotonin and oxytocin get released when we look into somebody's eyes.

As a stepfather, I had to fast-track some of my own parenting skills. I still remember the best advice I received when I moved in with Jen, and the kids were six and four years old.

My manager, Steve, suggested, "With all the travel you are doing with work, when you call your stepkids, make sure you are either sitting or kneeling at the equivalent of their eye level when you call and speak—don't pace. It will help reset your mind and remind you how young they are." (This is even more apparent to me today with my grandchildren. Equally, the "don't pace" rule is something I apply in adult phone discussions.)

Retired California Highway Patrol sergeant Kevin Briggs is known as the Angel of Golden Gate. He has saved hundreds of lives by preventing people from jumping off the bridge. I asked Briggs how important eye level is when speaking to people in this fragile state of mind. Here is what he said:

It really is important to understand that, on the bridge, where they are standing means they are below you. You're looking down on top of them. And I don't want that. I don't want to be looking down at someone. I would like to be at eye level, if at all possible.

When you're on your knees, it hurts. It's tough. It's brutal, because it's concrete... But sometimes you have to stand up, because as you get older, you're falling apart. I'm getting too many injuries. But it makes for a great connection. And you can be fairly close because that individual is here, just on your side of the metal beams.

You need to be able to communicate because it is so windy, and that traffic is going. It's critical to be at eye level with them.[5]

Not everyone will have the opportunity to listen in high-stakes situations. However, when you take the time to align at their eye level, the speaker will notice. When you connect and maintain eye contact during the conversation, you increase connection.

When it comes to eye contact, staring or gazing for extended periods of time can be interpreted as aggressive or intimidating. Keep your eyes in the triangle from their eyes to their chin. Focus on the triangle as an area, rather than exclusively and continuously on their eyes. You are looking and listening for patterns rather than for one-off eye moments.

Body language

Visual signals from the speaker are commonly referred to as body language. Consider this hierarchy as a way to start noticing body language, and when you feel comfortable that you have increased your awareness at this level, progress to the next: first face, then posture, and finally breathing.

Paul Ekman is the foundational scholar of body language—he has authored fourteen books and defined seven universal facial expressions: anger, contempt, disgust, fear, happiness, sadness, and surprise.[6] Ekman breaks these down much further into micro-expressions. These micro-expressions are influenced by facial muscles, including the eyes, eyebrows, nose, cheeks, and lips.

Throughout his work, Ekman reinforces that alignment between these facial and body expressions is the essence of reading body language. Don't become obsessed or fixated on individual micro-level body language signals; ironically, this will distract your listening. Notice the disconnect between what they say and how their face looks.

Notice the **disconnect** between what they say and how their face looks

I interviewed Susan Constantine, who studied under Ekman and has applied her focus in legal disputes and law enforcement. She reminded me of the fallacy of being fixated on one element of body language.

I really caution people [about] decoding others' body language without the proper training. The research shows that people are as accurate as flipping a coin when it comes to reading body language.

Even federal law enforcement, clinical psychologists, and federal court judges can't detect deception. They get very skewed because they're watching so many people lying to them that they assume everybody's lying. If they pick up on one clue, automatically they're lying.[7]

I want to reinforce that becoming an expert at reading facial expressions is a full-time job, and when it comes to noticing facial expressions, your role as a listener is to be present enough to see any disconnect between their face, their posture, their breathing, and what they say.

When working with my client Rachel, I noticed her body language and provided her a greater insight into what was said, thought, and meant. She was responsible for the merger integration of two different-sized companies. The acquiring company was four times larger than Rachel's company.

After three months of working together, we met up on the thirty-second floor of the central business district head office building. As the meeting started, I asked, "What would make this a great meeting for you?"

Rachel launched into a *familiar* pattern about the struggle around the merger integration, how no one understood how difficult it was, and whether she cared about the outcome. Rachel had created a story that it's unfair for the person from the acquired company to lead the integration—the acquiring organization should do it.

This dialogue continued for ten minutes, yet at the seven-minute mark, Rachel paused and took a deep breath; her spine and shoulders changed position, and then she continued speaking until she was exhausted by her own story.

I noticed the disconnect between what she was saying and her body at that seven-minute mark. I made a mental note to reflect this back to Rachel.

"When you took a breath, what happened?" I asked.

Immediately Rachel said, "Took a breath? When?"

Here, I could have replied instantly, saying something like: "At the seven-minute mark, when you said . . ." Instead, I paused and took a deep breath myself as I silently mirrored her body language.

In response, Rachel said, "I was frustrated with being frustrated; I paused and realized that I am draining myself of energy by rehashing this issue." She paused, then continued. "It's time. I can stay frustrated or change. Although that's not what I said, I had to verbalize every remaining excuse."

Finally, she said: "I want to move forward."

Ultimately, when you notice the disconnection between their words and their body language, it's not about you. It's about helping the speaker understand what has altered in their thinking. Be present to notice the disconnect between what they say and how it shows up in their bodies.

Visualization

I love collecting what people scribe when they listen to me. I regularly host an online community of practice with the Deep Listening Ambassadors. During these meetings, we focus on a specific and in-depth aspect of how to listen. What is fascinating about the infographics that follow is that they are notes taken by two different people listening at an identical time, in two different time zones and continents. Rebecca Jackson and Heather Willems were the scribes. You will notice overlap and differences.

First, take a look at Rebecca Jackson's notes. She uses a range of icons and verbatim notation. The key theme of the discussion—similarities and differences—is represented with apples and pears. There is a high ratio of words to images and limited use of empty space (negative space). There is a deliberate use of sequence and linear representation of the development of the ideas discussed over time.

Heather Willems's notes, meanwhile, use a range of visual imagery. There is much more empty space on the page, and ideas carry different weight based on the prominence of each idea. When Willems thinks of listening to herself, she uses a mirror, whereas Jackson draws an image of herself. Willems creates two columns with three bullet points that are blank when representing similarities and differences, whereas Jackson utilizes the fruit imagery—apples and pears.

It's important to understand that you don't need to be a scribe to capture the essence of the conversation. It can be as simple as three words in a discussion, or a circle, or arrows. All that matters is that it makes sense for you and becomes a prompt for your memory.

Ultimately, two people listening to the identical words can create completely different meaning based on their experience, education, culture, and profession.

Sense: Listening to and for emotion

Sensing emotions is the next step. Every discussion has emotion present. In fact, emotion is present in everything a human says and does. It's a signal to the listener about how they express the idea and what matters most to them.

The hazards of labeling

Be careful when it comes to labeling the speaker's emotions. If you have not mastered listening to yourself, this could lead to you labeling your feelings as their emotions.

Your focus is to notice when their emotions change rather than fixate on one specific feeling. The change in emotions points to something that matters or that has moved the speaker.

Avoid labeling the emotions of the speaker. This can be hazardous to the discussion and to the relationship. In a therapeutic setting, in the hands of skilled professionals, labeling the speaker's emotions has proven value. This takes years of training and practice.

This book is for workplace listening, not therapy.

Invite them to label their emotion. Remember my client Rachel? When she drew in that deep breath, I was tempted to label what happened. It would have been easy for me to say, "It sounds frustrating," or "I sense anger," or "Are you frustrated?" or "Are you okay?" All of which might have been accurate, yet not helpful for Rachel.

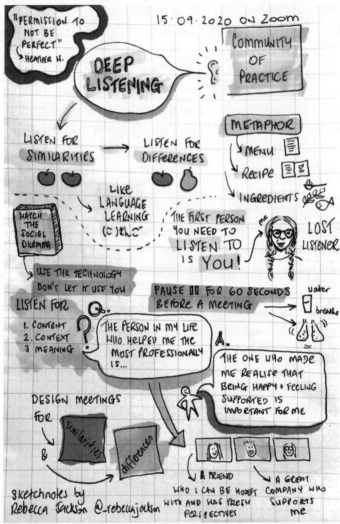

Visual notes by Rebecca Jackson from an online Deep Listening Ambassadors workshop

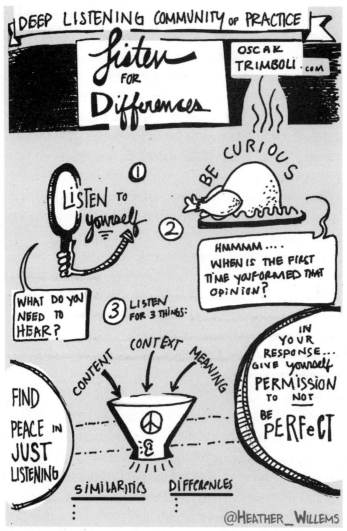

Heather Willems's notes from the same online workshop

If I had said, "You sound frustrated," this could be counterproductive. Labeling the person with the emotion carries a different weight in the discussion. The speaker doesn't need to carry the burden of your description of their feelings.

Holly Ransom is a professional master of ceremonies (MC) and has interviewed a wide range of people: presidents, prime ministers, and government and business leaders from across the world. I asked her what she listens for when interviewing global leaders. She said that she listens for their energy and for how much conviction they seem to have in what they're saying. From there, she told me, she listens for "a sense of how well they know themselves, and the things that they stand for."[8]

Emotions have a range and are always present; the mastery is in acknowledging their presence. A skilled listener will sprinkle in an invitation for the speaker's self-reflection during the discussion. Apart from creating a moment of self-reflection, it is also helping the speaker notice their feelings, which will help them explore their thoughts and meaning more deeply.

Tracking mood

Marc Brackett, founder of the Yale Center for Emotional Intelligence, has made his life's work the study of emotions in schools and workplaces. He has published many research studies and books on the topic. Here is what he told me about how emotion can affect students, and how paying attention to that helps him teach:

The speaker doesn't
need to carry the burden
of your **description of
their feelings**

If I don't know how my group is feeling, I'm losing information... For example, if half my students come into my class
stressed out and overwhelmed and scared, I know as a
researcher how their brains are operating in that anxious
state, and it's not in listening and learning mode.

Everyone should be a curious emotion scientist as opposed
to a critical emotion judge. And the emotion scientist is in
learning mode, not in knower mode. The emotion scientist is
open, not closed; curious, not critical.[9]

Brackett has created an app called the Mood Meter
(MoodMeterApp.com) that helps you label your emotions.
The app allows you to sort emotions into four categories:

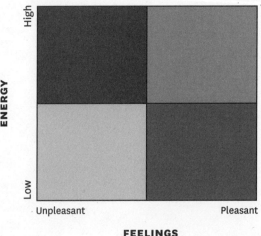

Emotions bring energy
to a conversation. **You** can
use their power to create
something compelling.

Each quadrant allows you to explore a range of twenty-five specific emotions and to place them in a home, work, or other context. It then invites you to reflect on your current mood and to decide if you would like to stay with your current mood or choose a different mood. Finally, it provides a helpful suggestion about how to move from the current to the desired mood.

Brackett says that most people's emotional language is sad, mad, and glad. The Mood Meter application has been a powerful tool to increase my own emotional vocabulary. The daily practice of explicitly describing a feeling has increased my emotional fluency.

Your role as a listener is to notice a change in emotion. Reflect on the change to the speaker and discuss whether exploring the sentiment is productive. Make the implicit explicit. Decide together if or how to discuss the emotions present or absent. Emotions bring energy to a conversation. You can use their power to create something compelling.

Note-taking

Taking notes when you are presiding over a person's liberty is one of the most consequential types of listening. In a court setting, many forces are competing for attention: legal precedents, each party's advocates, the media, and the weight of history. Michael Kirby, a retired justice of the Australian High Court, developed a pragmatic approach to note-taking:

When I was actually preparing for exams, I built tree diagrams with the major value or issue, and then the minor values, and then the sub-minor values, and the sub-sub-minor values in order that I could look at a page and see the whole page and see the sub-principles that I was trying to get into my head.

When I became a judge, I started by taking copious notes... but because, in the courts in which I sat, you got a daily transcript, it was a waste of time. Except... doing so helped get information into my brain.

There was a connection between my fingers, which were holding the fountain pen or ballpoint, and the writing of it to my brain and up into my cortex and into my memory.

Toward the end of my time on the High Court of Australia, I went back to the tree diagram. It was the way I saw the whole picture—because one of the problems in the law is getting transfixed with a particular text, either of an act of parliament or of a judicial opinion, and then forgetting the context of that text in the larger picture.[10]

The Deep Listening Research respondents highlighted that the speaker thought the listener's note-taking signaled better comprehension. Participants explained a range of note-taking techniques, including taking notes only about actions, taking notes about themes, capturing graphic notes, or taking detailed verbatim notes.

Note-taking is an intrinsic part of many professions—accounting, journalism, medicine, law, recruiting, and sales. Note-taking is part of the training in these fields and a quality signal to patients and clients that the professional is paying attention. Sometimes, these notes may even become evidence in a legal dispute. It can be an excellent way to summarize throughout the conversation and after the discussion.

A word of caution with note-taking: it will draw your attention and hijack your listening when you are in the process of scribing each word—verbatim. The speaker's speaking speed is much faster than your ability to capture word for word without losing your comprehension or place in the conversation.

A simple note-taking technique that you can use, if appropriate in the context, is to pause and say: "What you said is important. Do you mind pausing while I capture it?"

This process creates opportunities for the speaker and for the listener. For the speaker, they have the opportunity to understand that what they said made an impact. (Warning: in sales this might be perceived as false flattery.) For the listener, you have time to focus exclusively on note-taking rather than listening *and* note-taking.

Whether you are a copious note-taker or someone who relies exclusively on your memory, it is important to understand that the value of note-taking is as a shared document, which creates common understanding.

One of the critical aspects of note-taking is to ensure that the notes are shared or summarized for the speaker and listener toward the end of the meeting. I use the term *toward* the end—approximately 80 percent of the way through the meeting—not *at* the end. At the 80 percent mark, each participant can confirm their understanding or have the opportunity to understand where it diverged.

"When you focus on the writing instead of the listening, you tend to lose track and **the notes will not help**"

World memory champion and neuroscientist Boris Konrad explained the role of capturing information graphically and the difficulty with verbatim. He described workplace note-taking as "like stenography."

Make notes of just the important ideas mentioned: single words, maybe just a line to associate two topics that were related. It can guide your memory afterward. ~~When you focus on the writing instead of the listening, you tend to lose track and the notes will not help.~~

Very pointy note-taking—single words—can be very helpful. Do it every minute or two, just one word. This forces you to listen.[11]

When it comes to taking notes in my own work, I divide my listening into two distinct domains—*taking a brief* and *being in the moment.*

Taking a brief is used by professionals like accountants, dentists, designers, doctors, lawyers, market researchers, or physical therapists. There is a process when a potential client speaks to you for the first time, in which they describe their issue. The expert takes a brief through a series of questions, checklists, forms, and conversations.

I want the client to be thinking about these questions before we meet, so I share them in advance. This allows them to listen to themselves and the issues more deeply when they arrive. For example, I reorientate the speaker to consider questions about the audience and their outcomes rather than about my presentation or content. I ask:

1   Why is this event taking place?

2   Who is in the audience?

3   How does this element connect with the audience's experience before and after?

4   What do you want the audience to think, feel, and do—before, during, and after the presentation?

5   Where will the presentation take place?

6   What is the most significant barrier or risk to success?

7   What evidence of success will the event organizers notice?

By sharing these questions in advance, I am allowing the participants to reflect and consider before the meeting. Some people write down their initial thoughts in advance, and others don't. Either way works because I have provided a clear listening process for them.

Most people are surprised by how quickly a brief can happen when they have had the chance to reflect on the topic in advance and sometimes with others in their organization.

I capture one word or sentence for each question. Typically, the client is creating all the responses, so I have minimal need to capture anything other than to explore a range of perspectives, including others in the organization: employees, peers, executives, and stakeholders. Then we explore the impact of their ecosystem: their customers, citizens, competition, suppliers, regulators, and the media.

Broadening their perspectives helps the client listen in different and impactful ways. The client expects me to lead the process rather than the content. The content is theirs, and it can be narrow or broad depending on their purpose. I probably use less energy and take fewer notes than most people when I listen for a brief.

Being in the moment means focused discussions with one other person. The other format is group listening during workshops, presentations, or observations of leaders in action during their team meetings. These could be face-to-face, by telephone, or video conference. The topics can range from individual to group to organizational issues.

In all cases, I take either no notes or minimal notes—possibly a word or a sentence. This allows all my senses to listen to the speaker and the group. This approach allows me to notice what's said and, more importantly, what isn't said, either by the speaker or the group.

The implications of hear, see, and sense in an online world

Since 1996, I have been using, marketing, and selling video conferencing software. I have seen both a significant improvement in the technology and a disjointed adaption in human behavior in these forums.

During our Deep Listening Ambassadors Community meetings, we discuss practical workplace listening challenges and improvements. Community members reflect and discuss their struggles with hearing, seeing, and sensing in audio and video conferences.

The room you are in
will influence your listening.
Choose a room to match
the energy of the meeting.

As a result of listening to the Community of Practice, we created an additional resource called "The Ultimate Guide to Listening during a Video Conference" (OscarTrimboli.com/VideoConference). What follows is a summary of the guide's most effective tips for listening in an online environment.

Hearing tips

Whether at work, home, or in a third place, the room you are in will influence your listening. Choose a room to match the energy of the meeting.

If you are in an office or shared space, and if you have a choice, use headphones while listening to a video conference. This serves two purposes. First, it creates a ritual for you as the listener. The act of putting headphones on is a physical cue that your presence is required. Second, it signals to others in your location that you are focused elsewhere. It may deter others from interrupting you or from being noisy nearby.

Seeing tips

There are three dimensions to seeing during a video conference—your eyes, the speaker's eyes, and the eyes of the audience.

Group or "gallery" view is a default in video conferences. Rather than accepting this default for every meeting, choose instead to use the "speaker" view, saving the "gallery" view only for when it is needed. Watching the faces of every member of the audience is draining and creates fatigue.

In a physical meeting room, your eyes and body will occasionally scan the room and return to focus on the current speaker. In online meetings, with the distraction of every participant as the default view, your listening effectiveness is lessened.

Ensure that your webcam is as close as is practical to your eye level. It helps you and them. Your posture will thank you for having your webcam at eye level. It will reduce your physical and mental fatigue and provide more energy to listen.

Next, move the active speaker frame as close as possible to your webcam, and size it to be as close as possible to the actual size of the speaker's face in real life, rather than allowing it to dominate the screen. This may mean reducing the speaker image by 25 to 50 percent, depending on whether you are using a large monitor or other device.

Your video conferencing software will likely have accessibility functions, including closed captioning or live transcriptions. As a host, turn these functions on and announce their availability to participants. This will help you and the participants reduce the fatigue of catching up or keeping up.

If the spoken language isn't the native tongue of all participants, closed captioning will provide additional support and opportunity for them to see the spoken word and revise their understanding of what they heard.

Finally, have some fun when you get distracted. Notice the color of the active speaker's eyes. It will give you something different to focus on and reset your attention.

Sensing tips

Many video conferencing systems offer a series of emoticons to help participants signal to the host—speed up, slow down, thumbs up, celebrate, hand raising, and a vast range of graphics. As a meeting host, encouraging participants to use these icons can help you listen to the emotions of the online room.

Simple short questions can be illuminating for the host and the group. When posing these questions, consider the purpose of the question and its alignment with the purpose of the meeting. Be deliberate about your choice of questions, whether they are designed to help an unfamiliar group connect, invite self-reflection about an element of the meeting, or articulate a challenge or desired outcome.

Questions that are concrete and specific can be particularly helpful for groups that are new to each other. Abstract questions, meanwhile, can be useful when the group is close and has extensive shared experiences.

Specific questions might include:

- What is one thing you would like to achieve in this meeting?

- What is one thing you think this group needs to focus on in this meeting?

- What is one resource this group requires?

Abstract questions might include:

- As you come into this room, what color does the feeling here remind you of?

- What sort of drink are you feeling like coming into this room?

- What sort of music are you feeling like coming into this room?

You can pose these questions at the end of the video and ask people to comment on the difference—this can provide a non-threatening way for people to express how they feel and how their feelings might have changed during the video conference.

Using see, hear, and sense together

Most people primarily focus their listening on hearing. This is a wonderfully important foundation to listening. Remember that your ears and eyes are about the same height on your head. The alignment between your eyes and the speaker's eyes creates the ideal foundation for listening.

See the difference between what they say and how they say it. Notice alignment and congruency between their language and energy. When you notice a difference between their words and their energy, become more curious.

As you improve your hearing and seeing, move to sensing. Your role is to notice substantial changes in the emotions rather than focusing intently on every emotion.

how to listen this week

1   ~~Adjust where you sit during group meetings. Experiment and sit in different locations during the week and notice how this influences your listening—whether face-to-face or via video conferencing.~~

2   In group meetings, keep a count of the number of times people ask clarifying questions before answering the speaker's question, compared to when they answer the question immediately.

3   With your trusted workplace listening buddy, practice note-taking during a discussion. Every two to three minutes, capture one word, phrase, or idea each.

P.S. Thinking about the workplace listening colleague you chose in chapter 2, are you noticing more about how others are listening to you? Keep practicing with your workplace listening colleague—and remember: listening is a contact sport.

chapter 5

explore the backstory

---

*Great listeners influence
how speakers tell their story.*

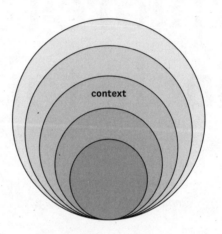

I DISCOVERED THE POWER of being curious and rewinding to the origins of the story firsthand while listening to community organizer Simon Greer.

The topic of the interview was Greer's project Bridging the Gap. This project is about teaching university students the communications skills they need to listen when they fiercely disagree with an idea or point of view, rather than simply talking back at the other person with their own ideas. This is an important difference that I need to regularly remember personally.

My opening question was this: "Simon. We'll spend a bit of time talking about Bridging the Gap. Before we do, do you mind taking me back? What was the conversation that sparked the idea to create it?"

Here was his response:

It's always dangerous when you're asked "take me back," because I could go back to when my parents came to the United States on a boat. They came from England in 1965. And to really understand me, you have to understand the part of the Jewish left that I grew up in.

I grew up on the Upper West Side in New York City and Man-
hattan, when it was still pretty working class, middle class...
pretty heavily Jewish and left. I went to a summer camp
called Camp Kinderland.

And when I say this to people, [that] it was a Jewish communist summer camp, they reply, "Oh, you mean liberal?"

No, no, I mean a Jewish communist summer camp.[1]

This backstory creates an entirely different perspective about
Greer, the project, and his part in the project. You understand
his history and its circumstances. Later, he revealed more of
his parents' story. They fled Poland around World War II to
arrive in England. After college, this came full circle when
Greer took his first job working for Lech Wałęsa and the Pol-
ish Solidarity movement.

This is the value of the backstory.

You and I feel like we know Simon Greer much better.

We understand how he has arrived at working on a project
about communicating when you disagree. We better understand his past relationships and their influence on his ideas
and his point of view when listening to disagreements.

With his backstory revealed, now it was time to build on
this foundation and the connection to explore the Bridging
the Gap project. Now, and only now, could I understand how
this project fits into his background and worldview.

Not all speakers commence the story at the beginning.
Rarely will they outline each scene, with all the characters
and their parts, into a coherent sequence. When the story's content is close or personal, speakers tend to start the

conversation from *their* opening scene rather than from *the* opening scene. When speakers explain the history of an issue, project, relationship, and the connected struggles, they will rarely explain it fully. They typically describe where they are at in their thinking, rather than the events. When they say it for the first time, that is the story in their mind, not the complete story.

Yet something powerful and transformational happens when a speaker says the entire story out loud from the beginning—from the idea's inception. ~~Verbalizing all the components of the story to all the participants creates meaningful connections for the speaker and the listener. It creates shared understanding and meaning.~~

The crucial movie scene

I am about to describe a movie in two different ways. Both are accurate explanations of the same movie. Each creates a different experience of the context and backstory. I would encourage you to read the first description completely and then the second description completely.

DESCRIPTION 1
The police interview a TV quiz show contestant.

DESCRIPTION 2
Salim and Jamal Malik and their mother live in Mumbai. When Jamal is five, their mother dies during a riot. The orphaned brothers flee, and later they team up with Latika—a girl who lives on the streets of Mumbai.

After a few years, Jamal and Salim become separated from Latika. Years later, Jamal finds work in a call center. His training teaches him a wide range of trivia and makes him the perfect contestant for a TV quiz show called *Who Wants to Be a Millionaire?*

Jamal wants to go on the quiz show because he knows Latika loves the show and will be watching. He arrives on the show and becomes a contestant—and, because of his training, he answers quickly and correctly. The host suspects he is cheating because of the speed and accuracy of his answers.

The love of Jamal's life, Latika, is watching on her TV.

While the show is airing, the local police are waiting to speak to Jamal. At the end of the penultimate round, the police commence an interview with him to investigate possible fraud.

They are trying to understand whether Jamal is a brilliant quiz contestant or an elaborate and sophisticated fraudster.

Full versus brief descriptions

Description 1 focuses on the crucial scene—the movie's climax. Although it is brief, it is an accurate, clear, and powerful description of the scene's essence. It has you leaning forward and wanting to know more about the TV quiz show contestant. How did he get into this situation? You want to learn more about the choices he made in his journey to arrive at this moment.

Description 1, despite its brevity, is common. Because people think faster than they speak, they explain what matters the most or what is front of mind. Their explanation seems clear to them, yet it may not be for others in the discussion.

This description makes it difficult to anticipate, appreciate, or understand the scene, the character's issue and his relationship to the police, the sequence of the movie plot, the heroes and villains, or ultimately how you connect with the movie's meaning. While the scene is the peak moment of conflict, most might view the essence of the film as more about romance and aspiration.

Yet this is like many conversations in which the speaker initially only describes their most crucial scene. Unconsciously, they ignore or eliminate the story's critical characters and elements. They reduce each participant's history into a brief moment rather than provide the full context.

If that's all you listen to, you are left trying to form connections utilizing assumptions, imagination, and interpretation. Now the speaker has planted the seeds of confusion, and you have become distracted.

There are two distinct perspectives of a backstory: what happened in terms of actors, events, and relationships (the backstory), and how each person views and explains their role relative to others (their backstory). Your role as the listener is to listen to the backstory, their backstory, and their place in the backstory.

Invite the speaker to explain more from behind the scenes.

When you go behind the scenes, no one will be making assumptions or inferences. Participants won't be jumping to conclusions about which information is absent from the past or from the story's purpose.

Something powerful
and transformational happens
when **a speaker says the entire**
story out loud from the beginning—
from the idea's inception

When you hear, "The police interview a TV quiz show contestant," this could refer to many quiz shows, including *Take the Money and Run*, *The Dating Game*, *Bullseye*, or many others. Right now, there are TV quiz shows in your mind that I haven't mentioned, and your context and history are influencing which shows are present in your mind.

The narrow description provided creates a wide range of options. The background doesn't explain which country, which TV quiz show, or if the description is of a movie or of the quiz show inside the movie. Is the quiz show contestant being interviewed about something they did on the show or about something else? Your mind becomes a pattern-matching machine in the absence of the broader backstory.

Body language expert Mark Bowden explained it this way:

When you're listening, you have to bring in a whole context to really get closer to the meaning of things.

Our brain is not a knowledge machine. It's a best-guess machine. It's the same with our listening capacity. When we're decoding language, we're doing our best guess at what the decoding of it might be.

Sometimes we're so accurate at how well we've decoded it that we believe that we know the language. We believe that we know what they said—but we guessed what they said, and we guessed right.[2]

Listening is demanding and draining when the backstory is opaque and unclear. Now, let's explore what happens with a fuller description that incorporates backstory.

Description 2 helps you understand the connections that created the current scene and why it is crucial. It allows you to explore and understand the scene's relevance and meaning. What did you notice about arriving at this movie from the two different descriptions?

If all you knew about the movie was the critical scene, you would miss out on the relationships between the characters, not understanding the plot or the importance of the police interview. Without the backstory connecting the characters, the story's purpose, nuance, and meaning are hidden.

When you read Description 1, you may have thought, "How can I guess this movie from one sentence?" Yet many listeners arrive at a conversation listening to the speaker describe the climactic scene first, without any context, because that is how the speaker chooses to explain it. As the listener, you don't understand why actors are laughing, sad, crying, or angry because you don't have the background of the opening few scenes.

Rather than being honest and asking the speaker to rewind to the beginning of the movie, we think that being polite and using our clever pattern-matching mind will fill in the gaps. As Mark Bowden would say, we are using our "best guess."

This is an ineffective, inefficient, and energy-sapping way to join the dots. Your mind will drift and wander as it anticipates, hypothesizes, and speculates. This creates high costs for the speaker and the listener.

It's impossible to understand *the* backstory without the speaker fully and thoroughly verbalizing *their* backstory. The speaker's backstory is their role in the story, not the story itself.

Invite the speaker
to **explain more from
behind the scenes**

Shortly we will explore how *the* backstory connects to *their* backstory and why it matters. But first, if you did not recognize either of the movie descriptions that began this discussion... they both describe the 2008 Oscar-winning movie *Slumdog Millionaire*.

Pause and rewind

A pause and rewind during the discussion can be the most impactful way to listen. With your intention as a listener aimed at honest and curious transparency, you can ask the following questions to help the speaker commence their story at a more appropriate starting point:

- "When did you first notice...?"

- "When did the project/issue commence?"

- "Do you mind taking me back to the beginning?"

Exploring the backstory is designed to help them and you understand the origin of the story, along with each actor and their connection.

The backstory is about listening first *for the* backstory and then listening *for their* backstory.

Listening for the backstory is critical to help the speaker connect with the story's past events, milestones, and characters. Asking the speaker to go back to the beginning creates a shared understanding.

When you ask the speaker for the backstory, it helps them fully explore past events and connections that they may have avoided, forgotten, or skipped, or to understand and appreciate a different perspective with the passing of time.

The backstory needs to start at the beginning—at the very beginning of the issue—not where the speaker commences.

Start the story together

Consider the world's longest river. The Amazon is 4,000 miles long and has over 1,100 tributaries, of which seventeen are over 600 miles long. There are lots of places to start, connect, and progress when it comes to the story of the Amazon.

The Amazon River could be the story of Spaniard Vicente Yáñez Pinzón. He is credited as the first European to see the river, which he first spotted in March 1500 when he was almost 200 miles out to sea and noticed that the vessel was surrounded by freshwater.

A different backstory of the Amazon could be another Spaniard, Francisco de Orellana, who in 1541 navigated the entire length of the river. And yet another backstory could be about the Marajoa people of the island of Marajó, which the Amazon River surrounds, who inhabited the island from 400 BCE to 1600 CE.

Whichever place you choose to commence in the backstory of the Amazon, each creates an entirely different perspective about the people, events, and culture in that time and place. It could be about where the river starts or ends, or about the Indigenous inhabitants. It could be about individuals or a community. Either way, where you choose to commence the conversation is a deliberate choice rather than a default description.

When you think about the story's beginning, you see many places to start. A skillful listener will probe for the backstory most beneficial for the speaker to ensure the conversation is clear and connected.

When your attention is out, and you are giving attention to the backstory, you will know where and how to explore and when to pause and expand. When it comes to the backstory it is always better to err on the side of going too far back rather than not enough, or not at all.

Let's consider this together for a moment. Think about a recent situation with someone that might have been complex, confusing, or possibly a conflict for you. How much of the other person's backstory has been shared or explored? Ask yourself whether there is something you think they may have left out. For example:

- Could they have started a little further back in the sequence of events?

- When did they first notice the consequences of the issue?

- Did they explain all of the participants and their interactions?

If you were to take the opportunity to explore these questions with them, confusion, complexity, and/or conflict would be reduced. It's definitely worth asking them to explore more of the backstory.

Most backstories have lots of twists and turns and create deep and nuanced context, which creates a foundational shared understanding between all participants—past, present, and future.

The signal

It is September 8, 2018—a warm evening in Flushing Meadows, New York. It is the final of the U.S. Open tennis championship at Arthur Ashe Stadium. Serena Williams is playing Naomi Osaka. The atmosphere is tense, and the stakes are high for Williams. Tonight, she can become the greatest tennis player of all time, reaching twenty-four singles majors—matching a record that has lasted forty-five years. The match doesn't start well for Williams, with Osaka winning the first set.

At the beginning of the second set, Williams has won the first game. Osaka is serving in the second game, and the score is 40 to 15. After an extensive and draining rally, Osaka wins the point.

Chair umpire Carlos Ramos issues a code violation against Williams because her coach, Patrick Mouratoglou, is coaching her from the player's box in the stands. Coaching in Grand Slam tennis is not permitted during a match.

Williams approaches Ramos and says, "If he gives me a thumbs-up, he is telling me to come on. We don't have any code. And I know you don't know that and I understand why you may have thought that was coaching. I'm telling you it's not; I don't cheat to win. I'd rather lose. I'm just letting you know."

Fast-forward to the fourth game. Williams is ahead 3 to 1. Her frustration gets the better of her. She slams her racquet into the court. The chair umpire calls another code violation—a point penalty against Williams.

She is confused and asks for clarification. "This is unbelievable. Every time I play here, I have problems," she says.

The backstory needs
to start at the beginning—
at the very beginning of the
issue—not where the
speaker commences

From this moment on in the match Williams is distracted, and, despite being well ahead, she loses the second set, the championship, and the opportunity to claim the Grand Slam tennis record.

What can we learn from the backstory?

In tennis, a call of coaching is defined as "the umpire observing the coach sending a signal." The player does not need to see the signal for it to be defined as coaching. The player is penalized because the player is responsible for the behavior of the coach.

Umpire Carlos Ramos has a reputation for issuing coaching penalties. He had previously penalized Serena Williams's sister, Venus Williams.

In a post-match interview, Patrick Mouratoglou explains that he doesn't enjoy good eyesight and should be wearing glasses. It matters because he is unsure if or when he and Williams made eye contact. Mouratoglou admits in multiple post-match interviews that he was coaching Williams.

In one interview, Mouratoglou says, "I am honest, I was coaching. I don't think she was looking at me, so that's why she didn't even think I was. I was like 100 percent of the coaches on 100 percent of the matches."[3]

In the heat of the moment, with it all on the line for Williams to become the greatest Grand Slam player of all time, the backstory was everything.

The umpire's backstory is that he has a reputation for penalizing coaching, and Williams's coach was coaching, although it is quite evident that she didn't see it. With the full backstory, you can understand why Williams felt angry, frustrated, and betrayed.

The backstory is the critical link between fragments and connections, frustration and understanding, the obscure and the obvious. Ramos displayed a complete lack of empathy for the occasion and for Williams. He lacked genuine curiosity. His approach was robotic and inhumane. Rather than listening, he steadfastly and rigidly applied rules.

By continuing to adopt the power position, nearly seven feet above Williams in his chair, he accentuated the image of him talking down to Williams rather than the exchange being a meeting of equals listening at eye level.

When you are listening during a conversation, are you adopting the position of the player or the umpire?

Three questions to explore

Whether it's Francisco de Orellana on the Amazon or Serena Williams at the U.S. Open, the backstory generates nuance that helps connection and increases impact.

Paradoxically, the act of asking the speaker to rewind the story isn't designed for the listener. It's designed to help the speaker thoroughly and comprehensively explore how they understand *their* place in *their* story and how they relate to the larger story.

Here are three questions to ask to help them explore *their* backstory:

1   What was that like for you?

2   What did that feel like for you?

3   What were you thinking about at that moment?

These short questions help create a new perspective on how the speaker relates to the story with the passing of time. This will create a different context compared to the story they have told themselves.

Wasted water

Holly Ransom, whom we met in chapter 4, was part of an international women's leadership project in Korogocho, Kenya. She worked with twenty-two local women to establish a micro-finance project to stimulate sustainable economic self-sufficiency in the community. During her first week, Ransom toured their village. She explains:

In the first week we were there, there was a lot of due diligence —just trying to understand the culture, get a sense of the local market economy. We'd spent the morning with the tribal chief, and every afternoon we would wander to this big sea container where we would teach the women business skills.

About a kilometer and a half away from the sea container, we stumbled on what looked like a brand-spanking-new [water] well, which really struck me as odd, because we'd been told since we arrived in Korogocho that the women had to walk about three and a half kilometers every day to get fresh water. That was the closest source.

I said to our interpreter, "Hold on, isn't that a well?" And the answer came back, "Yeah, it's a well."

And I said, "Is the well broken?"

And he goes, "No, it's not."

The backstory
is the critical link
between fragments and
connections, frustration and
understanding, the obscure
and the obvious

I'm sitting there going: Hold on a minute. Here's this well that was built by an aid-development company using probably about $20,000 worth of aid money.

I just said, "Why aren't they drinking from the well, then?"

The answer came back: "The well was built on ancient battlegrounds. There's bad spirits in the ground. We can't drink the water from this well, or we'll end up with bad spirits in us, and we'll die."

I just remember sitting there going, "Wow!" Five hundred meters down the road... there is a well that could've serviced an entire village. But because there wasn't any listening on the part of the people that were coming in to help—and I believe they were doing it with the best of intentions—but because they'd imposed their version of things and hadn't listened to the people they were trying to serve, that unfortunately ended up so far off the mark of what they were trying to achieve, and who they were trying to help.[4]

The cost of not listening to the backstory is wasted human potential. Many projects in your organization might start in the wrong place because you don't take the time to understand how similar projects have succeeded or not in the past.

Here are three questions to help you explore the backstory of projects:

1   Have you undertaken similar projects in the past?

2   Who was involved in them?

3   What can we learn from their success or otherwise?

When you take the time to listen to the project's backstory, you will probably avoid many ancient workplace battlegrounds. Now, let's take all of these lessons and put them into practice.

Discover the backstory

Discovery commences with an invitation. There are many invitations you can use as you listen. Invitations are best posed as questions.

Compare *Where would you like to start?* to *Could you start at the beginning?* Both sound similar, yet each has a very different emphasis and orientation. Let's explore a little further.

Where would *you* like to start? The emphasis here is on *you*, and consequently the invitation allows them to make it all about themselves. This is an invitation for the speaker to explore and expand.

Could you start at the beginning? This is a broader question that allows them to think about the issue from a more comprehensive perspective than the story and their role. It implies the beginning of *the* story rather than the beginning of *their* story. These are very different locations for the speaker to commence.

Sometimes the speaker might become trapped and only be able to tell *their* story. When you notice the speaker getting stuck in their story, help them notice too. Stuck can show up as anxiety, frustration, or repetition. It can show up as excitement and as energy. Notice when the speaker starts to

The cost of not listening to the backstory is wasted human potential repeat elements of the story—that is your opportunity as the listener to become a little more curious about them and their language.

Your role is not to point out that they are stuck—your role is to help them notice if being stuck or repetitive is productive for them. It's important to ask "Do you notice a pattern?" when they are repetitive.

Don't label the pattern for the speaker. It's more powerful if they label their pattern. When they label their patterns, they will enjoy a moment of insight or a shift in perspective.

Being stuck and staying in a place of no progress can be a powerful location. It can be simultaneously comfortable and uncomfortable. Rather than attempting to emerge or progress, understand what is helpful whilst pausing.

We will explore more extensive ways of noticing language patterns in the next chapter, but for now, if I could leave you with one thing, it is this: *Remember that you are not an objective observer in their story.* Your presence in the discussion will change the speaker's awareness of the issue and their perspective, whether you choose to say anything or not.

Remember, listening is subjective. Your subjectivity is what makes you human. Great listeners are aware of this and claim it. It moves conversations from robotic discourse to human discussions and connections full of emotion.

The speaker will imagine and reimagine a different past, present, and future they haven't considered—exploring their assumptions. The backstory will create new meaning from their old stories. The speaker explores and sometimes discovers a new pathway for their thinking.

how to listen this week

1   During a discussion with one other person, ask the speaker: "Do you mind taking me back to when you first noticed this?" (This is a great exercise to practice with your workplace listening partner.)

2   During a group meeting, ask the speaker the same question: "Do you mind taking me back to when you first noticed this?"

3   In a group meeting, keep count of the number of times the speaker starts a significant explanation of the issue by commencing in the present rather than by outlining the backstory.

P.S. When you are thinking about group meetings in which you could practice listening for the backstory, consider this for groups with projects or issues that are in the first third of their lifecycle rather than something that is close to its conclusion.

Select groups where you have existing relationships, rapport, and trust rather than ones in which you are establishing a relationship.

chapter 6

notice how it is said

Words are the ingredients
and sentences their recipe.

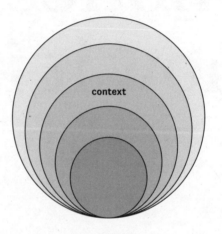

OVER MANY YEARS, retired police sergeant Kevin Briggs, whom we met in chapter 4, was typically the first responder on his motorcycle when someone was considering jumping off the Golden Gate Bridge in San Francisco. I was intrigued by how he listens to people in this state of mind, when the stakes are immense.

I'm speaking to so many people—I'm thinking to myself, "How would I want someone to approach me?"

I'm thinking, "Is this individual scared?"

This could be his last day on Earth: frightened, scared, or under the influence of alcohol or drugs. We don't know.

When I'm first walking up, I don't know what encounters they have had with law enforcement before, good or bad. I'm in this uniform, but instead of saying, "Hey, I'm Kevin Richard Briggs with the highway patrol," and walking right up on that thing, saying I'm coming in peace. I don't want to scare them.

"Can we have a conversation, just you and me?"

"I'm here for you. I don't want to see you get hurt."

He was feeling me out a bit. He didn't want to talk. At the start, most people don't really want to talk.

But you keep going with them and show that you care, and you have empathy: "Hey, what's going on?"

Eventually, he started talking and he could see that I was interested. And I'm giving him my full attention. And that's exactly what I did. I turned off my radio. I needed to be focused.

The whole world is in this little circle.

This is what's important.

He finally started trusting me, a little more, a little more, a little more, a little more.

And I could see he started using more adjectives and describing things more. He was relaxing just a little bit.

It took quite a long time before he actually started to care enough to hold on to that rail.

Especially when we started talking about his child—that was a big one for him, as it would be for anyone, and it should be.

So as this progressed, I could see he was breaking down some, and sometimes that can go either way.[1]

Briggs notices the increasing use of adjectives as a signal—a signpost of increasing trust. The speaker was open to the possibility of a living future and described what led them to this moment on the edge of the bridge.

Briggs is listening simultaneously to himself, the words, and how those words are being expressed. He can decode what is said and notice that the adjectives are clues. Adjectives are describing words. This helps you understand what and how they are explaining what's on their mind. It helps them describe what it means for them.

Speech and language offer a palette of colors. Colors have range, intensity, and vibrance. They can blend to form subtle and nuanced variations. They can also be black and white.

The same is true for a conversation. In chapter 4, I explained that you can be speaking in blue, they can be speaking in red, and the dialogue blends the two colors, forming purple. Like color, language has patterns, opposites, and combinations. When listening to the word patterns, you gain insight into how the speaker uses vocabulary to make sense of their world. Their speech pattern is how they translate the world into their unique words, sentences, and stories.

We will explore these patterns using the following categories:

Language: The syntax of the dialogue—adjectives and pronouns

Preferences: The way they portray their history and ideas

Time: Their relationship to the past, present, and future

Thoughts through language

Language is the way two or more parties communicate. It is a shared experience. It is formed, transmitted, and received. It does not exist in isolation. When people communicate using language, they're influenced by family upbringing, education, community, and culture, and, as a result, these patterns are unique.

Language has form and structure, and the key influencing factors are how people use adjectives and pronouns to describe their ideas. People use adjectives and pronouns in unique patterns. These patterns help you understand how the speaker relates to the issue and expresses their perspective.

This layer of language is like a regional accent or dialect. Although you are both speaking in the same base language, the way you communicate specific concepts varies subtly or dramatically based on the participants' familiarity with the dialect.

As the listener, you need to be aware of the adjective and pronoun patterns of the speaker; otherwise, the conversation could be laden with the weight of misunderstanding. This misunderstanding could lead to frustration. As a result, listening starts to take more effort and becomes less effective.

Adjectives

Adjectives are words that describe objects or issues. They typically describe nouns. Patterns in adjectives emerge in the way people describe issues. Adjectives might be used to explain the energy, shape, or size of a problem. Notice when adjectives form patterns, as it will provide an insight into the preferred communication style of the speaker.

A project is a group of people and resources with an expected outcome and time frame. Yet people can use adjectives to describe the same project in very different ways.

During a client assignment dealing with a six-month engineering quality improvement project, I was asked to assist the group in creating a shared understanding. I asked them to place one or two words into an envelope that described the project. These are the descriptions I read out loud to the group from the words in the envelopes:

The complex project

The costly project

The draining project

The duplicated project

The frustrating project

The high-profile project

The never-ending project

The political project

The unnecessary project

You quickly get a sense through the adjectives about where the gravity was in this project. As important as it was for me to understand their current state of mind, it was more important that the group understood how they felt about the project.

Adjectives are **signposts** for teams and systems

The adjectives described how everyone was feeling in relation to the project, rather than the project itself.

We spent the next ninety minutes discussing the shared understanding of how the group felt, rather than rushing to solve the issue and fix the project. At lunch, one of the participants asked me for a private discussion. She explained how revealing it was that everyone felt safe to tell the truth anonymously to a sealed envelope, yet there was not enough trust in the group to speak up and listen to each other.

She asked, "What do you think that is about, Oscar?"

I said, "Would you feel comfortable asking the group this question after lunch?"

She said, "No."

I realized I had much work to do and had only touched on the surface issues in the project. The list of words did not mention trust, yet every adjective pointed out the absence of it. The undiscussable was not being discussed—we will talk more about *the unsaid* in chapter 7.

If you know what to look for, it's possible to spot language patterns, even in a workplace setting. Anthropologists study cultures and patterns of human behavior, comparing universal and subtle differences in human societies, especially in the construction and expression of language and its patterns.

Michael Henderson is an anthropologist specializing in corporate cultures. To understand and explain corporate culture more effectively, he contrasts ancient civilizations and modern workplaces.

I asked him, as an anthropologist, what he listens for in workplaces. He told me that adjectives are "road signs" that can tell you which direction the person is coming from, or which direction the person is attempting to go in. "By listening to those adjectives repeatedly, you get a sense of their worldview," he said. "By listening very carefully to the language and repeated patterns, you can bring this to their attention."[2]

Adjectives are signposts for teams and systems.

Pronouns

Pronouns are linguistic shortcuts to describe someone. They may include *I, you, she, he, it, they, their, them, us*. Pronouns are useful shortcuts to understanding the speaker's orientation. In chapter 2, we described this as the location of their attention. When their attention is *in*, it's about me: I, my. When their attention is *out*, they are more likely to be using we or us.

The three layers of orientation to notice are me, them, or us. These will vary based on the issue and the relationship. The speaker can use pronouns that signal self (me), other (them), or system orientation (us).

- *Self orientation:* me, I, mine

- *Other orientation:* they, them, team

- *System orientation:* us, organization, community

Chase Hughes has trained many people in the defense, police, and intelligence services. He explained the importance of being aware of these orientations:

Whether you're watching *The Bachelor* or you're in a business meeting, listen to the words that people are using.

If I want to communicate better, I'm going to listen to the type of pronouns that you use.

I'm going to listen to whether you talk about self, teams, or other people. If I ask you, "Oscar, how do you like doing this podcast?" and you say, "Oh, it's great. I set my own hours. My work is fantastic," that's self pronouns.

If I ask you the same question and you say, "Running this podcast is great. I'm interacting with my fans on a regular basis. I've got a fantastic audio editor. We really work well together," that's team pronouns.[3]

Hughes's point is essential and straightforward. Rather than focusing on one or two specific pronouns, notice clusters and patterns across the pronouns. Listening for the pronouns will provide clues about how to ask questions that may create a different perspective.

If they're stuck in a monologue and you notice through their pronouns that it's a pattern focused on *me*, ask them a question from a different perspective: *we* or *they*. If it's a team or project that's stuck in an internal pattern, invite an external view—customer, competitor, citizen, or regulator. It could be in a different industry or country. Often, this will create the circuit breaker they need to listen differently to the next steps. Holding a mirror to their patterns can create an observation, insight, or a-ha moment, or it can reset the discussion.

Be careful: you can get lost or misread a situation if you become fixated on only noticing a narrow language component. It is a trap. Rather than analyzing every adjective and pronoun continuously, make it easier for yourself and just notice if they change the use of pronouns.

Listening to the patterns in their language—the adjectives and the pronouns—will help you maintain your focus when you get distracted.

Thoughts through preferences

The way we explain our issues is unique. Each person has a way of speaking that is as individual as their fingerprint. Life experience, education, and community participation influence how people talk and express themselves.

All artists have access to the same range of colors when they paint, yet it's their choice of colors, canvas, brushes, and emphasis that makes the painting uniquely theirs. The options extend to how to use color and the absence of color. It is a decision to paint in black and white or color, to be precise or abstract. It can be individual or collective.

The way they express their ideas will help you listen to the brushstrokes rather than to the colors in the description they are painting. When you listen at this level, nuance emerges. The speaker feels you are hearing the essence of what they are saying and that their thoughts and feelings are appreciated.

The range of ways an artist can express themselves is not limited to the canvas—they can choose sculpture and any other form of expression.

When you notice how
people speak, rather than only
what they say, you get a sense
of how they express themselves—
their unique communication
fingerprint

This is true for artists and writers. Writers can choose short stories, long stories, poetry, stage productions, movies, and so much more. Whether it's artists or writers or when you speak, you have a range of infinite possibilities to express yourself. As the observer or the listener, you can notice many patterns that help you make sense of what's discussed. Noticing the common patterns creates a shared understanding.

It would be a vast simplification to say that people either speak in stories or statistics, anecdotes or evidence, big picture or details. As humans we use a range of heuristics— mental shortcuts to make sense of the world—and narratives versus data is one way to notice how the speaker likes to express themselves.

You have a preference for one or the other. Consider it your primary listening filter or worldview. Sometimes, if there is a mismatch of communication styles in the dialogue, you may get frustrated and distracted. Sometimes, it can be the similar yet nuanced difference between their explanation and your experience of a common issue that might frustrate you.

Speaking patterns are unique. When you notice how people speak, rather than only what they say, you get a sense of how they express themselves—their unique communication fingerprint. When you recognize the pattern, listening becomes lighter and more straightforward. Alignment between how they speak and how you listen reduces friction in the dialogue, creating a sense of ease that allows both speaker and listener to relax and focus on what matters.

A word of caution: conversations can be quickly derailed, and not only by what people say or how they say it. Conversations can become a struggle because of mismatched communication styles. These examples from the Deep Listening Research highlight the impact on a speaker when their default communication preference is telling stories, but their listener's preference isn't:

- "Someone isn't listening thoroughly. They are more likely to interrupt during your explanation or story."

- "I feel like I must be a boring storyteller. So I stop trying to tell stories."

- "It's frustrating having to tell the story over again."

Each example references stories or storytelling. The pattern in this set highlights the value the speaker places on their story and their place in the story. By adjusting your listening presence for the storyteller, you will increase trust. The speaker will relax and reach their point faster because they don't feel pressured to get to the end. Listen to their complete story.

The next research example highlights what can happen when a detailed communicator experiences a mismatched listener:

- "Having to repeat important details multiple times."

- "Later asking for details or not getting the details correct."

- "I am wasting my time explaining important details that they need to hear."

- "They're not paying attention to the details."

- "They often miss important details."

They want you to notice and reference the details in the conversation. These types of speakers reference a lack of note-taking by the speaker as one of their most significant issues when noticing their comprehension.

As a listener, when you notice the speaker's primary communications preference and acknowledge their prefer-ence when you are paraphrasing, you send a huge signal to the speaker that you are listening to *what* they say and *how* they are saying it. Acknowledgment of their communication preference will remove the friction from the dialogue and increase the trust with the speaker.

Positive and negative preferences

Another pattern in the speaker's language you can notice while listening is how they relate to the issue. When they express the concept, do they explain the possibilities and the opportunities or the struggles and difficulties? Your role as a listener is to help the speaker notice the pattern rather than judge how they express it.

Earlier in this chapter, I described the sealed envelope exercise in which the participants in a project described it as a negative experience. In that moment, there might have been a temptation to rapidly reorientate the group back to the positive purpose of the project. That is not your role as the listener. Your part is to help them notice the pattern and then make an invitation: *How would you like to explore it?*

It's very alluring and seductive to fix, progress, or solve. Without the group acknowledging its current pattern, you could reduce trust and waste effort if they immediately attempt to move forward.

This is true for groups and for individuals. Be careful to announce your label for their language pattern—make the invitation to the speaker to create their label. When they use their own label, it helps them make progress in a way that makes sense for them. It becomes their insight and their decision, rather than something you suggested or said.

Absolute and relative preferences

Explanations as absolutes are a clear signal about underlying assumptions that the speaker is making. Absolute terms include *always, never, all, none, every, strictly, true, false, unique, precise, identical, necessary,* and *unconditional*, to name a few.

When you hear the use of this language, you are inside the thinking of the speaker. This is an insight into their mental models and narratives. When you understand the foundations of their thinking, you better understand how they make sense of their reality and how it will influence their future.

I was working with Lana, an executive at a professional services firm. She was incredibly frustrated about the performance of the division that was working with the public sector, versus the private sector division.

Lana said, "For the last three years, the commercial division has continued to grow. They have established a straightforward approach and focus on helping their customers, and, as a result, I will continue to invest for their success. The public sector division, on the other hand, is frustrating and anemic. They *always* struggle with growth. *None* of our team enjoys working with their bureaucratic ways. They lack a fundamental appreciation of how we can help them."

When you understand
the foundations of their thinking,
you better understand how they
make sense of their reality and how
it will influence their future

Lana finished with a final exhale. After a moment, I inquired with one word. "Always?"

Lana sat back in her chair, looked up to the corner of the ceiling, and collected her thoughts. The frustration moved from her stomach to her chest, past her throat, and out of her mouth. "Yes, Oscar. *Always, always, always,*" she said. "In the last three years and in my *entire* career, I don't see growth. *In fact*, Oscar, *every* public sector customer is *exactly* the same."

Again Lana paused, and I inquired, "Every?"

She smiled back and said, "Okay, not every one."

In that moment, I invited Lana to explore and play the Relative Game. I said, "Lana, consider *all* of the public sector customers. Imagine they are in this room, and in the far left corner are the customers who have grown and in the far right are those who haven't. What does each group have in common?"

This was the longest pause in Lana's thinking—it felt like five minutes, yet it was only thirty seconds.

Finally, she said, "For the customers on the left side, now that I have thought about it a little more, there is a subset of those who have bought more of our services than the private sector customers. Three customers in this left group have grown at 200 percent, and I have ignored them because of the public sector label."

I asked, "What do they have in common?"

Lana provided a thorough explanation about their growth profile, the markets in which they operate, the mindset of the leaders. Here, she made her decision to classify customers differently. She was open to other ways rather than grouping customers based on their industry—commercial or public sector. At her next team meeting, she asked her team if they might group their customers differently.

This insight emerged by listening to Lana's use of absolutes. The payoff for Lana was transformational, and her organization continued to grow with a different approach to the identical market conditions of the last decade.

Sometimes the speaker will develop a pattern around comparison relative to this, that, them, or others. Discussions will compare details, people, or systems. In the workplace, discussions about actual performance relative to budget is a common example of relative language. Another is comparing your salary relative to that of others in your organization, industry, or profession.

Your role as the listener is to notice their relative point of comparison and help them explore whether it is meaningful or mythical.

In my discussions with executives about salary and performance compensation ethics, they arrive armed with industry benchmarks, percentile bands, tenure, and job level data. The group concludes that this distribution of bonuses is an optimum way to reward performance and retain staff—one that is rational, mathematical, and defendable.

I will invite the group to calculate the cost of recruitment in the last fiscal period as a proportion of the decision they have just made on compensation. Typically, the information provided is vague and imprecise compared to the math of the last decision. Yet some in the group quickly realize that, relatively, they might be spending much more on recruiting and training compared to salary increases or bonuses. This often leads to an energetic discussion about compensation versus recruitment rather than a mindset of how to allocate pay increases and bonuses.

Traveling through time

Where the speaker starts the dialogue in time is another helpful clue about what, how, and where they are thinking. The speaker will explain the time of the situation, their place in time, and their relationship to time.

They will anchor their discussion from the perspective of the past, present, or future. They will attach themselves to a constant location relative to time. It's worth your effort as a listener to notice when they explain the issue in time. They will leave clues about where their thinking is initially located and possibly where they want to take it.

Examples of this are phrases including "As I look back at the situation, what I realized was..." or "I see that I need to look forward to improve..."

Wherever they orientate their explanation in time, you will need to notice where your preference is and whether that is creating tension for you and them.

If you prefer to discuss the past, they will be comfortable if they dissect and relive the details. If, however, you relate to time in the future and they don't, this may distract as you find yourself wanting them to speed up.

The way they explain events is one relationship they have to time. Another is how they think about themselves in time. When they present their role in the situation is another helpful hint.

When listening, notice how they locate the story in time and understand how they position themselves along a timeline.

Their relationship with time may be specific or loose. While assisting a British company in Mumbai, global cross-cultural expert Tom Verghese had to explain the difference between time as a concept in the United Kingdom in contrast to how it is understood in India.[4]

When explaining the concept of Indian Standard Time (or Indian Stretch Time) to his client, he had to reinforce that time is an approximate concept in Mumbai compared to in London. If the meeting is booked for the top of the hour, that is an approximation, not a start time. Without this knowledge, you could be listening in frustration as someone explains time differently from your understanding.

When you notice the mismatch in the timing orientation between you and the speaker, you have already made progress in your listening—well done. If you want to expand the speaker's time orientation, occasionally pose a question that signals to the opposite place in time, when these questions support and progress the agenda or the agreed outcome.

Take care when asking these questions—ask with curiosity and shared understanding rather than with jarring and disjointed questions. Pick one type of question and make it your own, rather than asking all three types of questions at once.

The following table suggests some possible questions to explore with a speaker who may be unaware that they are anchored to a time orientation that might be unproductive for the discussion and the agreed-upon outcome.

SPEAKER ORIENTATION	PAST	PRESENT	FUTURE
Who	Looking forward, who needs to be involved?	Who was there at the beginning?	Who was there at the beginning?
When	How far into the future do you want to explore?	How far into the future do you want to explore?	When did you first notice this?
Where	Looking forward, where would you like to go?	Looking forward, where would you like to go?	Looking back, where were you on this project?

Note how the questions you might ask are pointing to a different time frame than the speaker's orientation. These questions are designed to help reset and restart the speaker into a different orientation around time that aligns to the outcome of the discussion.

You now have a different perspective about listening to *how* the speaker says something rather than only what they say. Remember that words are their ingredients and sentences are their recipe. When listening to *how* they say it, keep in mind the three dimensions of *how*: their language, their preferences, and their description of time.

how to listen this week

1   Consider the list below and notice your own speaking prefer-
    ence first. Focus on one element of how you say it each day
    rather than identifying all three at once.

- *Language:* stories or statistics
- *Preference:* negative or positive
- *Time:* past, present, or future

2   During a group meeting, choose one speaker you know well.
    Listen and notice how they explain a concept. Focus on one
    element of how they say it during a meeting.

- *Language (stories or statistics):* count how many stories they
  use during the conversation compared to when they refer to
  evidence or data

- *Preference (negative or positive):* count how many times they
  refer to problems or solutions

- *Time (past, present, or future):* count how many times they
  use past tense versus future tense in their sentences

3   During a group meeting, choose an unfamiliar speaker. Listen
    and notice how they explain a concept. Focus on one element
    of how they say it during the meeting.

- *Language (stories or statistics):* count how many stories they
  use during the conversation compared to when they refer to
  evidence or data

- *Preference (negative or positive):* count how many times they refer to problems or solutions viewed from outside their organization

- *Time (past, present, or future):* count how many times they use past tense versus future tense in their sentences

P.S. The difference between hearing and listening is action. How did you do with listening to the backstory with your workplace listening partner?

chapter 7

focus on what is unsaid

*Meaning emerges in the silence
between the words.*

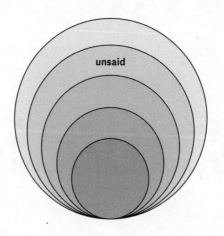

DANIELLE OFRI IS a primary-care internist at New York City's Bellevue Hospital and a clinical professor of medicine at New York University. I had the opportunity to listen to Ofri reflect on a patient who came to see her. She said:

A young woman wearing a baseball cap came in complaining about a fungal rash on her scalp. Very simple and easy to treat. Then she mentioned various aches and pains in different parts of her body and things that didn't add up to any particular syndrome. It was an elbow, it was a knee, it was the side of her thigh.

I examined her. She was perfectly healthy, and I said, "Yeah, just sort of the aches and pains of life," and, you know, "I'll see you next year" kind of thing. Then we said goodbye. She started to walk out, and I went back to the computer and started writing.

Then... she opened the door and was standing outside the room. But she didn't let go of the doorknob. She said, "Excuse me, doctor—can I ask you one more question?"

I said, "Sure."

She said, "Do you think that it matters... that all these aches and pains are spots where my boyfriend shot me with a dart gun?"

I realized it was domestic violence underneath all of this, and I had missed it.

When someone has disparate aches and pains that don't add up, you really do want to query about intimate partner violence. But I hadn't—I was really staying with the surface.

But she, luckily, held onto the doorknob and was courageous enough to stay holding on and to push one more time to get me to hear. Luckily, I caught it, because we know that these are people who become murder statistics so easily in these situations. And I was so grateful that she did this, and reminded me that I've got to always be careful to make sure nothing else is going on underneath.[1]

Listening to the unsaid is powerful because the speaker notices what else they are thinking, rather than only the first thing they say.

Listening for their unsaid is the most potent form of listening. Their first utterance is surface level—it's top of mind. It's the obvious and fastest thinking to access, yet it's not the thinking that creates insight or impact.

In chapter 3, you explored the differential between the speed at which someone talks and your listening capacity—the 125/400 Rule. They speak at 125 words per minute, yet you can listen at 400 words per minute.

Their complete thoughts are not in their first explanation

The speaker has a similar challenge. There is a difference between their speaking speed and their thinking speed. They think much faster than they can speak, and their thoughts are cloudy and disjointed in their mind; therefore, how they say it the first time might not be the most effective way to express the idea.

Your role is to become a book editor and consider the speaker as a writer. A writer has many words in their mind and many ways of expressing an idea. The writer's mind is a random collection of different concepts and many words. The editor's role is to get to what the writer is thinking about in the best way to express the concept—the essence rather than the first thing they write.

An editor encourages the writer through multiple attempts to improve what they write and how they write it. Each writing round progresses the idea and makes it easier for the writer and their readers to understand.

If we don't accept that what people write the first time is what they think, why do you as a listener only hear what they say the first time and assume it's what they are thinking? Their complete thoughts are not in their first explanation.

Speed of thought

The way that the brain processes language was discovered in the 1800s by French doctor Pierre Paul Broca—this part of the mind is called Broca's area. Harvard University researcher Ned Sahin used modern technology to measure the speed of thought and overlaid language processing syntax to determine that it takes the human brain 600 milliseconds to think of a word.[2]

If the 125/400 Rule is about talking versus listening, then **the 125/900 Rule** is the difference between the speaker's talking speed and their thinking speed. The average person will speak approximately 125 words per minute, yet they can think at a rate of 900 words per minute.

This massive difference between speaking and thinking speeds means that most speakers aren't saying what they think or mean completely if you only hear the first thing they say.

Here's another way to express it: the first thing the speaker says is 14 percent of what they are thinking. This means that 86 percent of what they think and mean is obscure and opaque to the listener.

The 125/900 Rule is the biggest insight my clients take from me about listening. Whether my clients are bank tellers; customer service representatives; salespeople; professional services leaders in advertising, accounting, legal, or technology; or executive or public sector officials, when I explain the vast difference between speaking and thinking speed, an audible sigh is heard in the room.

The speaker will ruminate on their issue or idea before they say it out loud. Their mind will be like a washing machine—murky, agitated, moving around from left to right, from top to bottom, seeking the best way to express what they are thinking. The wash cycle takes a lot of energy.

Speaking is like the rinse cycle for the mind. When you say something to someone else, it crystallizes *what* you want to say and *how* you want to say it. It's unlikely that what you say the first time is what you completely think or meant to say.

Even a washing machine has multiple rinse cycles to ensure everything comes out clean. When the speaker is saying something the first time, they will need multiple cycles to get out their clearest thoughts.

There are many elements of the thoughts and concepts that the speaker is struggling to express and explain. It takes time and multiple attempts to describe an idea or topic through speech. When the speaker ultimately describes it the way they *actually* think about it, you will notice a change in their state and posture. They will audibly exhale when they get to clarity. Some people call it the a-ha moment or the lightbulb moment. Typically, the speaker will draw in a deep breath and sigh, and then you will hear phrases like:

- "Actually..."

- "Also..."

- "Maybe..."

- "Now that I think about it a little longer..."

- "The most important thing is..."

- "What I actually want to say is..."

- "What matters most to me is..."

At this moment, the speaker is accessing what they want to explain and how they need to explain it. As the listener, your role in these moments is to create the space to allow them to access their thoughts rather than only what they said the first time.

Speaking is like
the **rinse cycle for
the mind**

"I thought it was obvious—we are a snake"

In 2015, I was facilitating a group of twelve leaders in a technology company in talks about the future of the organization. It was 12:30 p.m. and I posed a question to the group: if this company was an animal, what would it be? As we went around the room, the answers were very similar: eagle, falcon, hawk, cheetah, leopard, lion, and so on. And the explanations were consistently about speed and domination.

By 12:55, we had completed eleven of the twelve leader discussions about their chosen animals, and the CEO was tapping their pen on the table and indicating the time to me. Lunch was due in five minutes, and I sensed they were hungry—except there was still one person to go. Lyn hadn't explained her animal. In fact, she hadn't said anything all morning.

I nodded to the CEO, acknowledging the time and possibly the hole in their stomach. I was curious about what else was possible for the room if they heard from Lyn. Without a word, I turned toward her—rather than making direct eye contact. I reached out with an open palm toward her and said nothing, yet invited her to explore with the rest of the room.

In a careful and measured tone, Lyn said, "I thought it was obvious!"

Then, for a moment, it felt like she stopped—in reality she had simply paused, but it felt like a full minute as the silence filled the room and the tension on the face of the hungry CEO became more evident. They gave me a look that felt like they were sending a laser beam out from their eyes to explode my head. Patiently, I gestured to Lyn to continue.

"I thought it was obvious—we are a snake."

Pause for a moment and place yourself in that room. When you heard Lyn say "snake," what would have gone through your mind?

If you are from the West, the snake conjures negative emotions: slithering, slippery, untrustworthy, unexpected attacks. A snake is not something to be admired. Yet what you don't know about Lyn is that she is from China, and what a snake means to her is very different from the sneaky serpent characteristics of a snake in the West.

The tension in the room increased as Lyn continued with her explanation. She said, "We have forgotten to shed our skin like a snake each season. Our past skins are holding us back and we need to shed those skins from our past for our new customers and staff."

Immediately, the tension was released and the room exploded into a vigorous conversation about snake skins and what is holding back the business. Dated processes, systems, and mindsets not previously discussed were liberated by the mere mention of the snake.

The CEO and the other leaders found a new source of energy, and lunch didn't commence until 1:35 p.m. After lunch, completely different plans emerged because the group was patient enough to explore more opinions and perspectives rather than listening only to the initial consensus.

This is the power of exploring longer and not being fixated on discovering the correct or common issues, and instead being comfortable with navigating in an unknown direction that holds an unknown impact.

Taking the time to explore all the possibilities and all the voices in the room helped the company see many possible futures. When you always hear from the same voices and perspectives, it reinforces the obvious and known possibilities. Asking "what else" and "who else" generates multiple possibilities and opportunities.

Explore the gap

The unsaid in a group discussion amplifies if it is not carefully uncovered.

I am regularly asked to observe board and executive meetings for individual and group listening. In these situations, I notice that skilled hosts listen in two distinct ways. They notice who is speaking and who isn't, and they notice the topics that are being avoided, ignored, or left unsaid.

These influential meeting hosts don't wait until the end of the meeting to invite unspoken topics or individual opinions. They are regularly sensing if the gravity of the discussion is concentrated with a minority of participants. They are looking and listening to the room for a range of views. Often, people simplify meeting participants into loud and quiet. Yet when they listen for the presence and absence of themes, many dimensions emerge:

- Customers and shareholders

- Experienced and emerging

- Experts and generalists

- Financial performance and employee compensation

- Internal and external

- Long-term and immediate

- Policy and political

- Return on investment and loyalty

- Risk and opportunity

- Suppliers and innovation

- Spoken and unsaid

When you are hosting a meeting, the first place to start is to invite people who haven't contributed toward a discussion as early as is possible and practical in the agenda. Waiting beyond the 80 percent mark of the time allocated to a conversation is like forgetting to put yeast in your dough and then opening the oven door while it's baking. The result isn't the sum of the ingredients, because sequence and timing matter as much as those ingredients.

Like with a bread dough, a group's ideas need time to blend together, rise, and finally expand to their full potential. When you wait too long in a group discussion, you miss out on vital inputs. The result is flat and usually unappetizing.

How to uncover the unsaid

"How long have you been thinking about this?" and "When did you first notice this?" are powerful questions to help the speaker express what they have already explored in their mind but have yet to verbalize.

Treat silence like
a complete word: listen to
the beginning, middle, and
end of their pause

These curious and straightforward questions are profound because they allow the speaker two opportunities. One is to say something out loud for possibly the first time. Verbalizing will help them connect with their thoughts differently than when they are only speaking to themselves to explore the concepts in their mind. Your role as the listener is to help the speaker verbalize their ideas and issues in multiple ways and times.

In chapter 5, we discussed the importance of hearing assumptions. The loudest signal for assumptions is the use of absolute language. In chapter 6, we discussed the importance of noticing absolutes. Here is a quick reminder of these phrases:

- "Always"

- "Never"

- "In all circumstances"

- "Precisely"

When you notice their language preference, it is a coded message to explore a little bit further to uncover something that is not being stated.

Reflecting on their underlying assumption by repeating their *absolute* phrasing back to them will often be enough for the speaker to pause, reflect, and expand. They will explore what they are thinking more expansively. This starts the process of the speaker listening to their additional thoughts and meaning.

The unstated emerges when you invite them to express the idea with more details, depth, and nuance. This technique allows the speaker's language to catch up with their thoughts. If your primary listening orientation is time or solutions, you may experience the urge to fill in the space or complete their sentence when they pause. Acting on that urge narrows their opportunity to think comprehensively and thoroughly around the concept in their minds and how they want to express the issues.

Sensing what is unexpressed

Treat silence like a complete word: listen to the beginning, middle, and end of their pause. Silence is the unifying principle for what's unsaid. Silence is multi-dimensional. There is a significant difference between a pause that allows the speaker to catch up with their thoughts and the silence you take to understand what they just said.

English-speaking cultures have a confusing relationship with silence. Think of common phrases like:

- The awkward pause

- The deafening silence

- The intimidating silence

- The pregnant pause

In ancient and Eastern cultures, silence is a foundational part of communication. Silence is a sign of authority, respect, and wisdom. Silence is cultivated and embraced by elders and especially in spaces where groups gather.

Born in New Zealand, Vanessa Oshima moved to Japan in high school on an exchange scholarship. There she fell in love with her future husband, and with the people, history, and culture of Japan, and she never left. Oshima enjoys the duality of living in a country and culture in which she is considered a foreigner. Yet her passion for language and rituals comes from the perspective of an enthusiastic student. Oshima explained what she noticed about Japanese communications:

There are a lot of things in Japanese which are just unsaid, and so it's not directly said. You pick it up through the context, or you pick it up through the actions.

The famous one is when Japanese people suck in air when you say something, and they go, *hhhhhhhhh*. This means that you've really stepped over the mark.

The Japanese are wanting to say that listening and communication is just one step forward, one step back. It's an incredibly considerate culture. People stand in line orderly. In the trains, they don't shout and yell with their voice or on their iPhones. It's an incredibly aware culture of your surroundings.

The Japanese culture, the Zen culture, the Buddhist background can teach us about an awareness. Awareness of your surroundings. Awareness of the details. I think this is something that Japan can definitely teach about how to listen, taking in all of the aspects and all of the details.[3]

Silence takes many forms for the speaker and the listener. Using silence deliberately, intentionally, and purposefully will allow the speaker to collect all of their thoughts with coherence and clarity. The payoff for exploring silence is immense for the speaker, the listener, and the issue.

Pausing to notice their breath

In chapter 2, we explored how the deeper you breathe, the deeper you listen. It is time for you to pause and notice the speaker's breath. This is a layered and thought-provoking form of listening in which you notice where sound and speech commence in their body.

An elegant and skillful listener will notice the speaker's breathing and when it changes. They will notice where the speaker is breathing from, because it suggests how deep inside the speaker's mind, emotions, or body this idea has traveled. The longer and deeper the breath, the longer they have been thinking and reflecting on it.

Eric Arceneaux is one of the world's most influential voice coaches. He helps famous singers and many others to connect their voice, their breathing, and their identity. Here's what he explained to me:

I have a student who stutters really badly, and we were discussing how a big part of his therapy has not been vocal exercises per se or even breathing techniques... but just conversing with him and making sure that he had enough time to feel safe in knowing he was being listened to.

This can't be said across the board, but quite often certain vocal issues erupt from people's upbringings where they weren't given a voice or a chance to be heard. They begin to develop anxiety, and they become quite frantic in their attempt to communicate because they've felt like they've never been listened to.

When you feel like you don't have a voice figuratively speaking, you can lose your voice literally. There are issues like psychogenic dysphonia where people truly cannot speak, or [where] they're speaking as if through a vise. There's nothing physically or visibly wrong, but often it's from feeling like they haven't been listened to.

There are myriad vocal issues that result from people not being listened to.[4]

Arceneaux continued to explain how breathing impacts expression:

The average person thinks that singing works like this: you take a big breath and then you rush it out as hard as you can. You push it out and that's how power is done.

When [you] make sound, your brain sends the electrical impulses to your vocal cords to vibrate. But your vocal cords, they're very small and very easily overwhelmed if too much breath comes out of them at once—if you take a big breath and your body opens up. If you immediately collapse, your throat is going to be overwhelmed and it tightens up in response. I've learned that most people go to great lengths to not be present in their bodies. They're constantly trying to escape.

Arceneaux's insight for me was to notice where in people's body they are breathing from. Shallow or deep, constant or short of breath. When you are present to listen to their breathing and their words, listening becomes powerful for the speaker, for you, and for the discussion.

Listening to their breathing offers an early warning sign about what is coming rather than what has just been said.

Synthesizing themes

During one-on-one discussions, merely asking the speaker to notice any themes that are emerging will allow them to continue to summarize and explore their thinking a little deeper. Simple questions to pose include:

- "What themes are emerging?"

- "Are there any themes you haven't explored?"

- "Which themes matter most?"

In group discussions, you can safely and elegantly surface unexplored themes by inviting reflection. Paradoxically, these themes are often best summarized by participants who haven't spoken.

- "Could you summarize the themes?"

- "Which themes or perspectives remain unexplored?"

- "From the perspective of the customers, suppliers, or regulators, which themes require more discussion?"

Listening to their breathing offers an early warning sign about what is coming rather than what has just been said

The unsaid in organizations

Although we have focused on one-on-one and group discussions, the themes also emerge when listening at the level of organizations, communities, and ecosystems. When you need to listen to thousands and millions of people, this requires great care and respect in the way you ask and in how you show that you have listened.

Austin, Texas, is the eleventh-largest city in the United States. The Tonkawa tribes settled in what is now Austin, and today the city is famous for an annual film, music, and interactive entertainment gathering of over thirty thousand people called South by Southwest (SXSW). Hugh Forrest is the head of programming at SXSW and is responsible for listening to the audience's needs. He has to explore, locate, and curate ideas. He finds creators from the cutting edge of global creativity.

Forrest is listening for the future—an uncertain pursuit and one fraught with missed opportunities. This made me curious about how he and SXSW listen for the unsaid from people they will never speak to.

I asked Forrest to explain how to synthesize broad themes when he is looking around the corner or into the distant future. He says it starts with him and the team listening to audience feedback about the last event. They can't listen to thirty thousand people. But they can listen to what is unsaid by using thoughtful surveys and collecting themes. He explains:

Reading this feedback gives you a much better, fuller, and more nuanced perspective of what was good and what needs improvement.

The process of reading, digesting, and trying to understand feedback—of listening to what your users and what your community is saying—can be mentally, emotionally, and spiritually exhausting.

It's often not easy reading sharp criticisms of what you've done, particularly if you think you've done something incredibly great. Throughout the most harsh criticisms and the highest praise and whatever the objective truth is, it is somewhere in the middle.

We'll spend six weeks reading feedback, trying to analyze that feedback, trying to put that into some general themes and even more specific themes. Then, by about late May, early June, we're beginning to plan for the next year.

One of the big pieces in terms of planning for the next year is this SXSW Panel Picker interface that we've been using for approximately a decade.

This is an interface where anyone in the community can enter a speaking proposal. It's a system that allows us to listen to what the community wants, to get new ideas and new speakers into the event.

We'll get somewhere in the neighborhood of five thousand total ideas, speaking proposals, for SXSW, of which probably about a thousand will be accepted.[5]

When I heard Forrest say they take six weeks to analyze a vast ocean of feedback, I thought, "This is a mindset, not a job." It's an attitude about being curious and open. It's about making a change on a massive scale in the creative industries. This decade-long commitment has catapulted SXSW from a fringe event to a movement creating global change.

Many organizations constantly survey their customers, suppliers, employees, citizens, and others to provide feedback. Many organizations survey and summarize that information into themes, yet it's the rare organization that transparently communicates what they are actioning.

This ritual of the survey is a complete waste of time and money when the organizations collecting the information don't have a mindset of acting on what is communicated to them and communicating what they will do about it. It's a huge missed opportunity to hear what is unexpressed, unsaid, and then take no action.

What they think when they listen

Earlier, you met Vanessa Oshima from Japan, who spoke with me about market research being a listening profession. Oshima is a global expert helping brands like Nike, Coca-Cola, and Starbucks understand their customers and collect and communicate the insights. We discussed our shared love for marathon running and cancer research fundraising (our shared backstory). During our discussion, she mentioned something unexpected. Oshima had been diagnosed with breast cancer. She explained how her doctor communicated her diagnosis:

The curiosity to
pause and ensure shared
understanding will surface
what is unspoken

I'm really fortunate with my doctor. She's on the board of directors for Run for the Cure in Japan, and I raised a lot of money for Run for the Cure before I got diagnosed. She knew that I was running every day to raise money, and to raise awareness, and for my friend.

When I was first told, I had walked into the doctor's office, ready to get my test results. I had my husband with me, and I was expecting it to be good news.

"Oh, it's just this kind of benign lump." I'd convinced myself that it was going to be fine. I hadn't actually prepared myself for anything other than "Oh, you know, it's a benign lump."

My doctor needed to tell me my results. She just said, "So, you've got cancer." Those were the first words out of her mouth.

And I just went blank.

I just, I couldn't... It was like the air conditioning became really loud, and it was all just buzzing, and I couldn't understand.

And she'd gone into the communication mode of "So, the position where it is, this is what we need to do. You need to get your MRI, you need to do this, so we can determine the size, the spread."

And she was systematically going through what she needed to communicate to me, ticking off the boxes and sort of saying, "Well, the earliest we can get you into surgery, given the process we have to go through, is six weeks from now. That would be this date, are you free on this date?"

And I was still battered. "What do you mean, I have cancer?"

She had just moved on into fixing stuff, and I was still at "No, I don't have cancer."

My husband just grabbed my hand, and he was taking all the notes, and he was texting my sons. I just stopped listening.

I've learned a lot. When we're giving tough news, we're not actually being empathetic to the audience, to what they're coming into it from.

I think that's something I learned also through the cancer journey was that the doctor was charging through with her process of "I need to communicate this, this, and this to you"—just the way our market research report would be "I need to communicate this, this, and this to you."

And you're not even stopping to see if your machine-gun fire of insights, your machine-gun fire of steps for your cancer treatment is actually landing at all.

And that becomes really ineffective communication. So, in that sense, that means we're talking, but we're not listening.[6]

The curiosity to pause and ensure shared understanding will surface what is unspoken. When communicating complex or confronting information, the speaker is responsible for confirming with the listener that there is shared understanding.

The speaker and listener roles rapidly alternate during a conversation. Shared understanding can only be established if the speaker confirms what the listener heard, thought, and understood. Without a shared understanding, the rest of the conversation could be like two magnets repelling each other as polar opposites rather than attracting each other.

Michael Grinder, an expert in the use of language and questions, outlined how Oshima's diagnosis should have been delivered. He explained a linguistic technique called Three Point Communication:

Doctors are trained in high empathy. They will tend to lean forward as they're trying to say, "Thank you for coming," and they're saying, "I hate to tell you this, but you have X."

Now, that doctor is well intended, but that doctor is actually driving their message farther into you because of the eye contact.

Whereas if the doctor had said, "Now, thanks for coming. We're going to be looking at some x-rays," and then they turned and looked at the x-ray, especially if they used their arm closest to you, the listener, you'd be able to focus on the bad news and a third point, so that when the doctor came back and said, "And what we're going to do about that," the doctor would not be contaminated. We had separated the messenger from the message.[7]

In Oshima's diagnosis, the doctor and the message were immediate and not separated. The consequence is that so much that was unspoken was missed. The unspoken influences the relationship, the issue, and the outcomes. The doctor lost connection with their patient. Oshima lost her place in the conversation and spent a lot of time processing what was said, without listening to the next steps.

Rather than continue with the next steps, the doctor could have delivered the diagnosis and paused. "Do you have questions?" This takes a matter of seconds and helps the patient commence the process of taking responsibility for their recovery. The alternative was an extensive monologue by the doctor about treatment that the patient didn't hear or understand.

There are many simple, thoughtful, and straightforward phrases everyone can use to communicate complex, challenging, and confronting information. Such as:

- "Let me pause."

- "What sense does that make to you?"

- "What does that have you thinking?"

In this moment, you are simultaneously the speaker and the listener. Pausing in the conversation allows you and them to catch up with what has been said, establishing the launchpad for shared understanding.

When exploring their unsaid, these three phrases will consistently unlock their thinking. Allow the speaker to fully and completely express their ideas. When they pause, ensure they have completed speaking and are not simply taking a breath before they continue. You could disrupt the flow of their thinking if you inadvertently interrupt.

Ninja moves

When I deliver the Deep Listening workshop in-person or online, we integrate a simple exercise in groups of two or three. I recommend three people for this exercise.

I invite participants to reflect on a workplace issue they can immediately address in the next seventy-two hours, rather than something from the past. Each participant moves into a pair or triad and takes turns speaking for five minutes about the issue that they want to discuss.

Each participant enjoys the opportunity to take turns speaking and listening. Most people anticipate that they will find it difficult to speak on one issue for five minutes, yet when they are in the presence of a listener, they can speak beyond their allocated time.

Next, we outline the instructions for the listeners. They must listen in silence for three minutes—no interrupting, no paraphrasing, no clarifications, no questions of the speaker or the issue. Between the three-minute mark and the five-minute completion, the listener can only say, "Tell me more"—nothing else. No suggestions, no prompting for what they have already considered. Simply "Tell me more."

This exercise creates consistent insights and results, no matter the industry, organization size, country, culture, or context. The speaker's initial description of the issue is dramatically different to their final explanation. The speaker always generates more alternatives and solutions to their issues than they considered before the exercise. The speaker moves from vague to concrete actions and from problems to solutions by the end of the exercises.

For the listener, although initially agitated by the instruction for silence, they relax and enjoy the lightness of listening without any expectations on the part of the speaker. They notice their inner distractions faster and realize the importance of their presence when listening. Just listening changes the speaker's way of communicating.

These are the consistent patterns that emerge from debriefing the participants after completing multiple rounds of this exercise.

Speaker

1 They think that five minutes is too long. What actually happens is that the speaker uses all of their available time, despite initially feeling uncomfortable with the sound of their silence and voice.

2 They enjoy the opportunity to explore the issue fully without interruption—they find it energizing and refreshing.

3 The way they think and talk about the issue in the first three minutes is significantly different from how they think and talk about it in the last two minutes.

4 They generate at least three alternatives to those they have previously considered.

5 They say they have progressed the issue.

6 They know what it feels like to be heard and listened to.

Listener

1   Despite their feeling that this is an unnatural way to communicate, they are grateful to have a simple set of instructions and only one phrase to remember.

2   Initially, they notice tension in their minds and fight back the comments, questions, and distractions.

3   Around the two-minute mark, they become comfortable with no comments or questions and relax while they just listen—possibly for the first time in the workshop.

4   They notice that the speaker is generating multiple and different ideas that they previously had not considered.

5   They regularly check at the time as three minutes approaches because they want to say, "Tell me more." Some do and some listen in complete silence for the entire five minutes.

6   They are surprised that the speaker describes the issue from a significantly different perspective at the end compared to the beginning.

7   They realize that, when done this way, listening is not an energy-draining activity.

8   They appreciate that listening done well is not only about the listener understanding more of the content. It's about being present enough to assist the speaker in noticing their thinking and understanding their meaning.

SILENT and LISTEN
share identical letters

Of course, this is a training exercise, and in the real world not all discussions come with the trust and respect to set up a set of instructions for your conversations. Yet your willingness to pause a little longer creates a massive impact. It takes courage, empathy, and effort. The result makes it worthwhile.

If you don't want to find yourself robotically and continuously using the phrase "Tell me more," here are three alternatives you can integrate with your own situation and communication style. These three phrases transform dialogue when applied in full attention and with genuine curiosity and an open mind. Please don't ask these questions sequentially because you will create a sense for the speaker that they have not been heard.

The shorter the phrase, the more effective it will be for the speaker to explore their thinking and what they mean. Choose one and practice it:

- "What else"

- "And"

- "…"

The shortest phrase of all, the one that is hard to practice yet creates the most significant impact, is a complete pause— being silent just a little longer. During the group exercise I just described, a pause lasting three minutes created a material change for the speaker (and, quietly, it changed the listener's thinking too).

SILENT and LISTEN share identical letters. When I explain the 125/900 Rule and how to listen for the unsaid during workshops, I can see light bulbs turning on in people's minds. The change is profound.

Once I explain this magic trick, participants start to take notice of how many times I use these three phrases during the remainder of the workshop. Now armed with this knowledge, they can see the stage and the behind-the-scenes view of how to listen for the unsaid. For the remainder of the workshop, participants smile or giggle when I use these three phrases.

Despite knowing the magic of the phrases, participants continue to engage. They realize that the purpose is to help them thoroughly explore what is on their mind. It balances the power in the discussion and allows the speaker to take control of their issue.

Become present to and curious about what's absent from conversations.

how to listen this week

1   During a discussion with one other person in one meeting each day, ask any of these questions:

- "And?"
- "Anything else?"
- "Say more?"
- "Tell me more?"
- "What else?"

2   During a discussion with one other person, pause longer than usual before speaking.

3   During a discussion with one other person, pause until you are uncomfortable before speaking.

P.S. *The difference between hearing and listening is action.* Are you noticing that these exercises are building on the foundation of the previous week? Did you notice whether there is a bias for stories or statistics in your organization during last week's meetings?

chapter 8

listen for their meaning

Your role as a listener is not to understand what they say, but to help them make sense of what they mean.

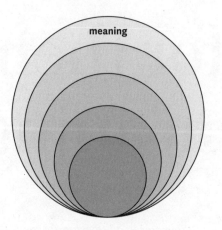

KATHY LEMAY HAS led an extraordinary life creating change for women around the world, in war zones or in their daily conflicts at home. At the point when I listened to LeMay, she had raised an astonishing $175 million for women's causes. She credits this to listening for *meaning*, not *money*.

LeMay shared a story from her early fundraising days in her twenties in New York City, when her friend Sue said, "Kath, go meet my friend Linda and tell her about this initiative." Here's what she said happened next:

I get the phone number and I call the assistant to this woman. We have a conversation and she realizes who I am and says, "Okay, great, we're confirming breakfast with you and Linda."

And she says, "She'll meet you at the Four Seasons Hotel in New York."

I get to the Four Seasons and I'm waiting and in comes this woman—and she is looking around in that way [when] someone's looking for you.

But I think to myself, "Oh no, no, no." There's no way this person can be my appointment because this is for women's human rights group and this woman walking in has big hair and a lot of makeup, a full-length mink coat, and incredibly tall stiletto heels, and I thought, "No way."

And she walks right over to me and she says, "Are you Kathy? I'm Linda." And she looks at me and she says, "Can I tell you why I was late today?"

And I say, "Yes."

And she says, "One"—and she takes her hand starting at her head and kind of takes it down her whole body and back up—"it takes a long time to look like this, and I have my husband's reputation to uphold."

And I just freeze, kind of thinking, "Oh my God."

And she says, "And also our friend Sue told me that you're awfully smart about all of this, and I was a little intimidated to come today."

And I say, "Instead of pulling out a pack and talking to you about the group, can I ask you how you know Sue?"

And we talk and I listen. And my goodness, she has had this life. I feel so ashamed of myself that when she walked in, I had made assumptions about her, because I was wrong.

She is smart and interesting and she tells me that when she grew up in her household, she and her mother were the only females, and at dinner every night her father and her brothers would talk about the social issues of our time and she and her mother were not allowed to speak.

She says, "I need women's groups as much as anyone does. People think because of the resources I have, I don't need them."

And she says, "I want to invest the money that I have because I don't want any other girl to be silenced the way that I was."

At one point, we are having this great conversation and I ask her what she meant about having to uphold her husband's reputation by what she looked like.

And she is giving me this glimpse into her life, which has been exceptional, and I am doing the same in return. And at one point she opens her bag and pulls out a checkbook.

She says, "So, how much would you like?"

And I say, "Do you want to see the pamphlet?"

She goes, "No—you can give it to me later, but not really. I just wanna be a part of what you're doing."

And I say, "Well, it's $10,000 a year for three to five years."

She says, "Great." She writes a check for $10,000 and hands it to me and asks me to write in the "to" line details.

And I say, "I will indeed," and she says, "Just so you know, you could have gotten much more."[1]

"I want to invest the money that I have because **I don't want any other girl to be silenced** the way that I was"

It's not the money that mattered to Linda; it's what the money represented. "No other girl should be silenced the way that I was." That meeting at the Four Seasons Hotel meant something entirely different for Linda. It was about community, connection, resources, and mutual support.

It's powerful when you create the capacity in yourself and the speaker to express the essence of the issue or idea. If you can help them listen to themselves a little longer, reflect on what it represents to them, and connect their past with their aspirations for their future, it will change their mind and the rest of their life.

The speaker creates their meaning when they link the past and the future. It's your role as a listener to help create this connection.

While listening for the meaning, your perspective moves above the dialogue and the discussion. You start to become aware of the energy and interaction between the speaker and the listener. You treat the conversation as another participant to be conscious of during the exchange.

Reimagine your perspective: let it move from two participants in a ballroom dancing together to the role of a spectator observing from above. In this state, your mind flows continuously through three perspectives without losing orientation, and it stays entirely in the moment. This flow feels effortless and detached from being about yourself, the speaker, or the situation.

This helps the speaker alter and reimagine the backstory, their narrative, and the possible future. It allows them to access this change where they are experiencing it: thoughts, feelings, or words. As the listener, you need to adjust your presence and questions to meet them where they are and explore what it means to and for them.

What it means for others

Bronwyn King is a lung oncologist, and many of the cancer patients she treats arrive because they have been smoking for most of their adult lives. She needs to explain the painful diagnosis to her patients and their families. The patients' cancer often takes a devastating toll on their relationships, their work, and, ultimately, their life.

King was buying her first home and met with her financial adviser about life and income protection insurance. She thought it would be a routine meeting. But this meeting was about to become life-changing—for her and for the lives of millions of smokers.

It was 2010, and I had a sit-down meeting with him to find out how much money I had in my superannuation [401K] account, and how that was going to impact the amount of money that we could borrow from the bank, and then which house we were planning to buy.

He brought along some paperwork and showed me how much money I had, which wasn't very much. We had a little chat, and then the meeting finished. I stood up and I shook his hand, and I walked away.

Completely as an afterthought, I sort of rushed back to the table and just said, "Oh, by the way, am I meant to tell you what to do with that money?"

The speaker creates their meaning when they link the past and the future

He said, "No, no, no, it's all taken care of. You're in the default option."

I just thought, "Hang on. *Option*. Does that mean there are other options?"

He looked at me and he rolled his eyes. "Look, there is this one 'greeny' option for people who have a problem with investing in mining, alcohol, or tobacco."

I said, "Did you just say tobacco?"

He said, "Yes."

My mind was sort of racing.

I said, "Does that mean I'm currently investing in tobacco?"

He said, "Yes."

I just thought, "That doesn't make any sense."

He said, "Well, look—everyone is."

I can't remember exactly what happened, except that I had this little moment right there where I thought I've been coming to work every day for about ten years trying to treat people suffering directly as a result of that product.

And whilst the community is very complimentary and kind toward doctors, the truth is that we don't have good treatments for the vast majority of people who suffer from tobacco-related diseases.

Most of them died because of that tobacco-related disease.

And so there I was, fully aware of the true impact of tobacco and seeing it in front of my eyes all the time, and then *this man had just told me I own shares in the companies that make the products that were killing my own patients.*

It was just this incredible moment. I thought, "I cannot let that continue unchallenged." And I guess the way that he said it made me realize that he wasn't particularly fussed by it; that's just what it was.

Whereas for me, I was very fussed by it. I was very concerned about that. I thought that was a glaring problem that needed to be addressed.

I thought, "I need to have a crack at fixing that."[2]

For the next decade, King traveled worldwide, visiting retirement fund managers, superannuation funds, government leaders, sovereign wealth fund managers, and insurance companies, listening to their boards and executives and becoming instrumental in divesting billions of dollars in shareholdings from tobacco companies. She has a compelling TEDx talk explaining her journey.

King created a global organization called Tobacco Free Portfolios and is now preventing more people from getting cancer than she could ever have treated as an oncologist. She will impact people in the world's emerging economies—the fastest growing smoking markets—because she thought about what her financial planner said and what it meant not just for her but for generations who are yet to be born.

Feelings and emotions create a rich and nuanced signal toward meaning

Although her financial planner was not listening to her, King heard what it meant for her and had the consciousness to understand its global and intergenerational consequences. She transformed lung cancer treatment, the finance industry, the way people invest, and the lives of millions of people and their families forever.

The role of feelings

Listening for the speaker's meaning requires great presence when you are sifting through the words and thoughts while noticing their feelings. I am often asked, "How do I help the speaker take their emotions out of a conversation?" I'll simply reply, "Emotions are another form of content to listen to." Often this question is more about the listener's comfort with processing their emotional reaction, rather than the speaker's.

Feelings and emotions create a rich and nuanced signal toward meaning.

Ken Cloke is the author of over thirty books on the topic of conflict resolution through mediation at home, at work, and across communities. He deals with complex negotiations about the locations of dams and mines, prisons and factories, and about homes, workplaces, and relationships. These mediations always have raw, intricate, and deep emotions present—yet nothing could prepare me for the emotion in this story that Cloke told me about the consequences of a dirty dish.

A couple comes to see me and we spend a couple of hours together and it's very useful. They walk away and they feel good about the conversation.

They come back a week later, and I say to them, "How has it been this last week?"

And he says, "Great."

And she says, "Awful."

Awful trumps great, so you can't say, "What was great about it?" You have to instead go and say, "What was awful?"

And she says, "Well, just this morning, as we're leaving the house, he left his dirty dish in the sink."

And he rolls his eyes, has a huge sigh, and says, "I can't believe you're bringing that up."

And she says, "Well, that's just like you to pay no attention to what I want or to the things that I object to."

And now they're off and running. The argument goes on and on.

They're getting into this huge argument, and the emotions are getting very hot, and the thing that they're arguing about is a dirty dish in the sink, and those two things don't match.

If they don't match, it means there's something else other than just the dirty dish in the sink, and the other thing is the meaning of the dirty dish in the sink.

I say to her after they've argued a little bit, "What did it mean to you that he left his dirty dish in the sink?"

And she says, "It means he doesn't respect me!"

Okay, now that's significantly more important. You can understand why somebody would get upset not so much about a dish but about respect. But this even doesn't go quite deep enough, because I can tell from their argument that this has touched a deep place inside of her.

She's really upset about this and he doesn't get it, and so I say to her, "What does it mean to you that he doesn't respect you?"

And she says, "It means he doesn't love me!"

Okay, now we've got it.

The dirty dish in the sink doesn't just mean the dirty dish; it means he doesn't respect her—and because he doesn't respect her, it means he must not love her.

Now his mouth drops open because he can't believe that we've gone from this dirty dish to the fact that he doesn't love her, and so he's kind of stunned.

I turn to him and I say, "Is that right?"[3]

Cloke is present enough to notice that *great* and *awful* don't match, and he chooses *awful*. A quick reminder from chapter 5: notice that these descriptions are all adjectives.

Cloke is not avoiding, ignoring, or sidestepping the emotion in the conversation. He is skillfully and elegantly noticing, holding it, and then leaning into it. He creates an invitation for the couple to explore the emotions bubbling around the words, so that they can discover what's below the words.

Next, Cloke uses a technique called laddering up. Rather than accepting the first response—*He doesn't respect me!*—he invites her to reflect up to the next rung on the ladder. He asks, "What does it mean to you that he doesn't respect you?"

This is an elegant example of neutral paraphrasing. She accepts the offer and moves further up the ladder. She says, "It means he doesn't love me!"

In the moment—in that room—imagine the emotion and tension. Yet, rather than pause and wait, Cloke continues up the ladder, turning to the man and saying, "Is that right?"

This is an existential question about the relationship and what it means, and it has nothing to do with the state of cleanliness of the dish. The meaning emerges through persistence, courage, and patience during the discussion.

This is not without risk. If done in a judgmental and careless way, the consequences could be catastrophic for the individuals and for the relationship. Use this rule to guide you in the moment: check back in with yourself and ask, *Is this about me as the listener, them as the speaker, or the conversation we are discussing together?* Meaning can emerge for you, for them, and for both of you. When listening for meaning, the typical sequence the speaker will explore is:

- First, what it means for them personally

- Next, what it means for them and their relationships with others

- Finally, what it means for them and for others in the context of the issue being discussed

If your question or intention is about you, make sure you notice it. As a listener, questions from your perspective aren't wrong. What you need to notice is whether it is helpful to you, the speaker, and the outcome you are seeking to progress.

Find the essence behind what is said

I have curiosity about Asia, and as a vegetarian, I find that many Asian cuisines cater well for my taste. The food is flavorsome, layered, and nuanced.

One of my favorite Japanese dishes is agedashi tofu. Dashi is broth distilled to the essence of the original ingredients. The actual components can include kelp, sardines, tuna (or shiitake mushrooms for the vegetarians) in hot water to create an exquisite layered broth. This process takes hours and a great deal of mastery—never too bland or too salty. The ingredients make a stunning stock that has your tastebuds noticing salty and subtle flavors.

Dashi is the essence of the meal. Listening for meaning is about depth, texture, and nuance. Tofu creates contrast in textures and flavors. Dashi is the distillation of the original vegetable flavors. You can easily distinguish each element in the broth. The dashi is served in a small bowl, with the amount of broth that would fit into a small teacup. Too much liquid and the dashi will lose its flavor and impact. Despite its modest physical presence, it has a flavor profile that lingers beyond the first taste. Although tofu, shallots, and fried onion shavings surround the dashi, the broth is the essential element of the meal.

When listening to
what the speaker is saying,
notice the surroundings, yet
focus on the essence

When listening to what the speaker is saying, notice the surroundings, yet focus on the essence.

Jennifer MacLaughlin is a deaf interpreter using sign language, bridging the gap between deaf and non-deaf communities. MacLaughlin is a world-class communicator and has mastered the flow of being available for the speaker, the listener, and the dialogue. She explained that sign language is three-dimensional and that meaning can be communicated much faster than by the spoken word. As a result, deaf culture and its communication style are more direct and to-the-point compared with non-deaf communities.

This may create misunderstandings on occasions for non-deaf speakers, especially in groups. MacLaughlin interprets the essence of communication—its meaning rather than every single word:

Finding meaning with interpreting... it's not the words. When interpreting for politicians, there is just so much faff on top of everything they say.

When I'm interpreting for a politician, they might start speaking and there are so many roundabout ways you can start a speech.

This might sound something like:

We've all... we've noticed...

There have been quite a bit of things that's happening in the space...

There's been a really big shift that's been going...

And I'm waiting, "Okay..."

I can stand there and wait. I know that they're generally talking about change, but I don't really have enough to commence. I can't start something, that's very clear.

I find managers of big companies or banks tend to look over at you like:

"Are you not meant to be signing right now?"

You have to stand there, because obviously you don't want to insult anyone. But they don't realize that they haven't said anything yet.[4]

MacLaughlin makes a great distinction between words and meaning. When she is signing, the purpose and intention is to communicate the essence, the primary point, rather than the words surrounding the conversation. MacLaughlin and the deaf community can teach the non-deaf community so much if it was open to listening. Focusing on the essence ensures that communication is clear and, more importantly, that any consequences are immediately surfaced and discussed.

When you are listening for what the speaker says, focus on the essence and work with them to confirm the core of their meaning in fewer words. They will speak in what visual scribe Anthony Weeks (whom we met in chapter 3) called "capital letters," and notice words like *actually*, *what matters*, or *the point is* to help them emphasize their meaning.

In that moment, they have said what they mean. Your role is to notice it for the speaker and the conversation. Here are a few suggested phrases and questions to help you explore for meaning:

- "What is important for you?"

- "What is essential for you?"

- "Where do you want to focus?"

Paradoxically, noticing the essence will take a little longer yet you will both arrive at the outcome faster.

Number matters

There are 155 people on board US Airways (Cactus) 1549 on Thursday, January 15, 2009, at 3:25 p.m., taking off from New York's LaGuardia Airport en route to Charlotte, North Carolina. This flight will create a whole meaning for everyone on board and beyond.

Below is the transcript of the one hundred seconds of dialogue between the pilot and the air traffic controller (ATC).[5]

> **ATC** Cactus fifteen forty-nine turn left heading two seven zero.
>
> **Pilot** This is Cactus fifteen thirty-nine hit birds lost thrust in both engines returning back toward LaGuardia.
>
> **ATC** Okay you need to return to LaGuardia turn left two two zero.
>
> **Pilot** Two two zero.
>
> **ATC** Tower, stop your departures. Got emergency returning.

Tower Who is it?

ATC It's fifteen twenty-nine. He—he, uh, bird strike. He lost all engines. He lost the thrust in the engines. He's returning immediately.

Tower Cactus fifteen twenty-nine, which engines?

ATC He lost thrust in both engines, he said.

Tower Got it.

ATC Cactus fifteen twenty-nine, couldn't get it to you. Do you want to try to land runway one three?

Pilot We're unable. We may end up in the Hudson.

ATC Johnny two seven six zero, turn left at zero seven zero.

ATC All right, Cactus fifteen forty-nine. It's going to be less traffic to runway three one.

Pilot Unable.

ATC Okay. What do you need to land? Cactus fifteen forty-nine, runway four is available if you want to make less traffic to runway four.

Pilot I'm not sure we can make any runway. Uh, what's over to our right? Anything in New Jersey? Maybe Teterboro?

ATC Okay, yeah, off to your right side is Teterboro Airport. Do you want to try to go to Teterboro?

Pilot Yes.

ATC Teterboro, uh, Empire... Actually LaGuardia Departure—got an emergency inbound.

Teterboro Hey, go ahead.

ATC Cactus fifteen twenty-nine over the George Washington Bridge wants to go to the airport right now.

Teterboro Wants to go to our airport? Check. Does he need assistance?

ATC Yes, he, uh... It was a bird strike. Can I get him in for, uh, runway one?

Teterboro Runway one. That's good.

ATC Cactus fifteen twenty-nine. Turn right two eight zero, you can land runway one at Teterboro.

Pilot We can't do it.

ATC Okay. Which runway would you like at Teterboro?

Pilot We're gonna be in the Hudson.

ATC I'm sorry, say again, Cactus?

Wow—all that in one hundred seconds. I wonder if you need to reread the dialogue to help make sense of it. While you were reading this, did you notice what was distracting you? Were there moments when you sensed the rise of your emotions or did you start to scroll through memories of turbulent flights or emotions in your mind?

Did you notice the inconsistent flight numbers?

1549

1539

1529

1529

1529

1549

1549

1529

1529

In many workplace discussions, participants fixate on numbers or exact details, which highlight inconsistencies or incongruity. Details can be very important until they're not. Details without meaning drain the energy of the listeners. Details with purpose can be an elegant way to communicate new ideas, or old ideas with new meaning.

Often in workplace conversations, executives and individuals become obsessed with counting the grains of sand on the beach, ignoring the tsunami wave approaching. The consequence is wasted energy and disconnected discussions, causing rework and frustration.

Back to Cactus 1549 and the flight numbers. The ATC and the pilot need to be precise with information sharing. People's lives are on the line. Present in their discussion are facts, details, risk, emotion, and consequences—every minor detail may matter. The implications for the passengers and the safety of people on the ground near the landing site are significant.

The US Airways Cactus 1549 flight number is critical until it is not. Despite the ATC and pilot getting the flight numbers wrong, the only number that matters is one five five. 155.

This is the very first number you read in this story. One hundred and fifty-five people are on board the flight—150 passengers and five crew. On that wintery Thursday afternoon in January, the only number that meant anything to the pilot, copilot, and crew was the number of people on the flight.

Unfortunately, focusing exclusively on the numbers and the detail misses what matters most in this story. I wonder what this story means for you?

Avoid the temptation to take control during the discussion. Things change, and your listening will need to adjust. The speaker may require a pilot, copilot, crew, air traffic controller, or passenger. Each role is valuable and may change during the flight. It is critical that you understand the role the speaker would like you to play. Sometimes they know, and most often they don't.

Simply ask the speaker: *How would you like me to listen or what would make this a great conversation?*

The questions help them become more conscious that the conversation is a shared experience, influencing the speaker to consider a broader perspective.

When you are listening for the meaning, elevate your perspective to that of an air traffic controller. Expand your viewpoint in the discussion beyond the participants—the pilot, crew, passengers, the plane, the airport, the runway, and the emergency services. Listen and watch from above and see the bigger picture: your role, theirs, and the surrounding airspace.

With this perspective in place, you can arrive at many destinations rather than one, which transforms the speaker's understanding as well as yours.

Three is half of eight

I interviewed Jennie Grau and her son Christopher about listening across the neurotypical/neurodivergent spectrum. This completely changed the way I think about listening. Grau said:

Chris has taught me a million things about becoming a better listener.

When he was three, he came home from school all excited about something, and he sat down, and he told me, "Mommy, three is half of eight."

And I was so distressed, but I put on my mother hat, and I said, "Hmm, let's explore that." I took out the M&Ms, and I put them on the table, and I put eight M&Ms on the table.

I said, "Chris, show me how three is half of eight."

And he looked up at me with the most loving eyes. And he said, "Oh, Mommy, you will never see it that way."

He grabbed a sheet of paper and a pen. And he created an eight, and he did a vertical bisection of the number eight. And he showed me the right-hand half.

And he said, "You see, Mommy—three is half of eight," with this giant grin on his face.

And I realized that the whole world was about to change for me because this kid was going to open my eyes to all kinds of things that I had not seen, had not noticed, and were going to become important.[6]

What Christopher said and what his mother heard were vastly different. His mother was listening to what Christopher said, not what he meant. This is true for you. Many people arrive at a conversation with a fixed perspective that *only four* is *half of eight*. As though anything else is incorrect—always—whether on Earth or on Mars: FOUR is HALF of EIGHT.

Every day in workplaces and homes, we participate in conversations by listening to hear what they say. Listening to confirm our educational, professional, and cultural understanding. We use their content to reload our point of view or argument and then shoot down what they said.

Do we entertain other possibilities? Are you fixated on your truth or on progressing the conversation?

Today and tomorrow, as you enter into discussions with layered meaning—for you, them, and a broader group or organization—please approach these conversations by asking yourself: *Is this what they are saying, or can I move beyond the words and sense what they are feeling or thinking and ultimately meaning?* What it means for them, for you, and for others.

When you listen for meaning, opposing ideas and views can coexist and cooperate. This is the essence of Deep Listening: impact beyond words.

When you **listen**
for meaning, opposing
ideas and views can coexist
and cooperate

My final thought for you to explore is that 3 is half of 8, 4 is half of 8, and 0 is half of 8. The symbols—0, 3, 4—mean everything, and ultimately they mean nothing. Be open to this possibility when listening; rather than obsessing about *one* way or *the* correct way, be open to listening deeply. Be confident that multiple points of view, opportunities, and outcomes will emerge. When you understand how to listen, you discover the hidden key to better communication.

how to listen this week

1   In a group meeting, count the number of times the speaker uses these phrases:

- "Actually..."
- "Also..."
- "I wish..."
- "Maybe..."
- "Now that I think about it a little longer..."
- "The most important thing is..."
- "What I actually want to say is..."
- "What matters most to me is..."

2   In a conversation with one other person, notice the number of times the speaker uses these phrases:

- "Actually..."
- "Also..."
- "I wish..."
- "Maybe..."
- "Now that I think about it a little longer..."
- "The most important thing is..."
- "What I actually want to say is..."
- "What matters most to me is..."

3 Ask a trusted workplace colleague to spend five minutes explaining something they struggle with at work. At the end of the discussion, explain what you thought the essential issue was to them—what it truly meant.

P.S. Practicing each week with these exercises will help you to develop more listening muscles. Each of the three tips to practice each week are simple. The effort is practicing. You can go back at any time and work with your workplace listening partner on each exercise, rather than only when you are reading this book.

over
to you

IN THE MOUNTAINS near Kobe City in western Japan is the village of Mikage. It has abundant water, delicious rice, and a climate that creates the perfect ingredients for making saké—Japanese rice wine. Kanō Jigorō was born into this region and the tradition of saké makers. Kanō means "production of delightful saké." Yet because his father was adopted, neither his father nor Kanō would become saké makers. As a result, they moved to Tokyo, where Kanō studied philosophy and economics. Kanō studied these subjects from three perspectives: Japanese, Chinese, and English.

Unfortunately, his academic success made him a target for bullies on campus and in the surrounding streets. In the 1870s in Japan, learning self-defense was a complex tradition integrated into Samurai ways. For Kanō, learning self-defense was easier said than done.

He discovered a series of teachers who taught him an integrated and modern form of jujutsu, which eventually branched off to become judo. Kanō became immersed in these ways. Eventually, he became a teacher with many hundreds of thousands of students, and through his long-term lobbying efforts, judo eventually became an Olympic sport twenty-six years after his passing: in 1964 for men and in 1992 for women.

While jujutsu was created on the battlefield by warriors, judo was created for peacetime. Although judo contains all of the jujutsu techniques, its emphasis is placed on throwing.

Kanō introduced the system of the Dan. The Dan is a signal of progress through phases of improvement and mastery at each level. You commence at white belt. Eventually, with consistent practice and progress, you may achieve black belt. At black belt, your progress is noted by the Dan: a stripe appearing on the belt—first white, and then red.

The modern system of colored belts (white, yellow, orange, green, blue, brown, and black) emerged as judo migrated from Japan to Europe in the 1920s. These additional colors helped Westerners focus on smaller, more incremental improvements toward mastery.

A judo player must show proficiency in eight distinct movements, defense, and response to progress from white belt. This proficiency emerges from the constant practice of eight basic steps under the supervision of a sensei—a judo teacher.

Practice and supervision with their sensei ensures the safety of the judo player. By focusing on micro-instructions and repetition of the task, the judo player can move from a rigid interpretation to a flowing movement.

The judo player practices in a dojo, and each belt level has clear and specific criteria. There is a clear definition of what is required to progress to the next level. The sensei will not ask the judo player to perform any kata (a form of movement) that they can't perform safely—either alone or with another person. Kanō said:

In an argument, you may silence your opponent by pressing an advantage of strength, or of wealth, or of education. But you do not really convince him.

Though he is no longer saying anything, in his heart he still keeps to his opinion; the only way to make him change that opinion is to speak quietly and reasonably.

When he understands that you are not trying to defeat him, but only to find the truth, he will listen to you and perhaps accept what you tell him.[1]

Maybe he was practicing *how to listen* when he said this.

Like judo, listening requires practice to progress. A focus on incremental improvement before you can move safely to the next level. A commitment to self-awareness and self-improvement. If you advance without mastery at the preceding stage, it's unlikely that you can perform consistently and effortlessly when listening at the next level.

Despite the urge to rapidly test higher performance levels, doing so could damage your progress. Kanō's mantras were "maximum efficiency with minimum effort" and "mutual welfare and benefit"—this is true for judo and for listening.

Listening is a contact sport, yet you can practice alone. Reading this book is a way to practice safely. Your listening will progress in every discussion and meeting—it only takes a moment of conscious awareness and presence. When you bring a mindset of being open to having your mind changed, the seeds of listening will flourish.

Listening is a sequence of moments, minutes, and meetings. Focus in the moment, and the entire conversation improves. When you focus on basics in the moment, your listening muscles strengthen and you can advance to higher levels of impact.

Throughout this book, you explored the art and science of listening. It is a practitioner's guide designed for your workplace.

Listening is a skill, a practice, and a strategy. Now it's over to you. The next steps rely on you practicing and improving how to listen.

Thank you for listening.

Oscar

About the deep listening research

The Deep Listening Research is a series of specific and ongoing investigations into what workplace professionals struggle with the most when it comes to their listening. Here are the questions that were investigated:

1 The Barriers to Listening in Your Workplace (August 2018, n=1,029)

- What frustrates you the most when someone isn't listening to you?

- What do you struggle with the most when it comes to listening to someone?

- If you could improve one thing about your listening, what would you like to make progress on?

2 Listening Barriers: Self-Assessment (September 2019, n=500)

- How would you rate yourself as a listener, compared to others in your workplace?

- Which of the following do you find most frustrating when

someone is listening to you? (Twenty questions on a five-point scale.)

- Is there anything else that particularly frustrates you when people aren't listening in your workplace?

3 The Deep Listening Quiz commenced in February 2020, and as of June 2022, 18,000 participants have completed the assessment.

- Twenty specific questions to establish the participants' listening barriers across four distinct archetypes: Dramatic, Interrupting, Lost, and Shrewd.

- Designed to capture age, gender, geography, industry, and professions-based data.

Notes

Your Invitation

1. Deep Listening Ambassadors Community, oscartrimboli.com/ambassadors.

2. *Deep Listening* podcast #067, "Making a Habit of Deep Listening with James Clear," oscartrimboli.com/podcast/067.

Chapter 1: Why Listen?

1. Jing-Bao Nie and Carl Elliott, "Humiliating Whistle-Blowers: Li Wenliang, the Response to COVID-19, and the Call for a Decent Society," *Journal of Bioethical Inquiry* 17, August 25, 2020, https://doi.org/10.1007/s11673-020-09990-x.

2. Xixing Li, Weina Cui, and Fuzhen Zhang, "Who Was the First Doctor to Report the COVID-19 Outbreak in Wuhan, China?" *Journal of Nuclear Medicine* 61, no. 6, June 2020, https://doi.org/10.2967/jnumed.120.247262.

3. *South China Post*, "Remembering Li Wenliang: The Wuhan Doctor Who Warned the World about Coronavirus," December 27,2020, scmp.com/news/china/article/3115445/remembering-li-wenliang-wuhan-doctor-who-warned-world-about-coronavirus.

4. Margarete Imhof, ed. "Listening Education," International Listening Association, January 2012, listen.org/submissions-listening-in-education.

Chapter 2: Get Ready to Listen

1. *Deep Listening* podcast #064, "The Art of Focus and Listening: Lessons from World Champion Shooter Christina Bengtsson," oscartrimboli .com/podcast/064.

2. *Deep Listening* podcast #093, "The Power of Listening and How It Forever Changed the Life of Heather Morris," oscartrimboli.com/ podcast/093.

3. *Deep Listening* podcast #060, "A Masterclass in Level One Listening: Listening to Yourself with Dr. Romie Mushtaq," oscartrimboli.com/ podcast/060.

4. *Deep Listening* podcast #074, "Unlock the Ancient Secrets between Listening and Breathing with James Nestor," oscartrimboli.com/ podcast/074.

Chapter 3: Give and Pay Attention

1. Raghuram Rajan, "Has Financial Development Made the World Riskier?" working paper 1172, National Bureau of Economic Research, November 2005, nber.org/papers/w11728.

2. Stephen J. Dubner and Raghuram Rajan, "This Economist Predicted the Last Crisis. What's the Next One?" *Freakonomics Radio Network* podcast, episode 366, February 6, 2019, freakonomics.com/podcast/ this-economist-predicted-the-last-crisis-whats-the-next-one.

3. *Deep Listening* podcast #013, "World Class Educator John Corrigan Explains How to Help Children Learn to Listen," oscartrimboli.com/ podcast/013.

4. Theresa Wiseman, "A Concept Analysis of Empathy," *Journal of Advanced Nursing* 23, no. 6, June 1996, https://doi.org/10.1046 /j.1365-2648.1996.12213.x.

5. Brené Brown, "Integration Idea: Empathy," Dare to Lead #DaringClassrooms lesson guide, 2020, brenebrown.com/wp-content/ uploads/2021/09/Integration-Ideas_Empathy_092221-1.pdf.

6. *Deep Listening* podcast #018, "Public Listener and Visual Scribe Anthony Weeks Explores the Canvas of Listening to Business and Community Groups," oscartrimboli.com/podcast/018.

7. Kittie W. Watson, Larry L. Barker, and James B. Weaver, "The Listening Styles Profile (LSP-16): Development and Validation of an Instrument to Assess Four Listening Styles," *International Journal of Listening* 9, no. 1, 1995, https://doi.org/10.1080/10904018.1995.10499138.

8. M.D. Phillips, M.J. Lowe, J.T. Lurito, M. Dzemidzic, and V.P. Mathews, "Temporal Lobe Activation Demonstrates Sex-based Differences during Passive Listening," *Radiology* 220, no. 1, July 2001, https://doi.org/10.1148/radiology.220.1.r01jl34202.

9. Jack Zenger, "Age, Gender, and Ability to Listen: Who Listens Best?" *Forbes*, June 11, 2015, forbes.com/sites/jackzenger/2015/06/11/age-gender-and-ability-to-listen-who-listens-best.

10. Shankar Vedantam and Mahzarin Banaji, "What Does Modern Prejudice Look Like?" KDLG Radio interview, April 22, 2013, kdlg.org/post/what-does-modern-prejudice-look#stream/0.

11. Oscar Trimboli, "The Four Villains of Listening," Deep Listening Research Insights, 2019, oscartrimboli.com/wp-content/uploads/2020/01/villains-research.pdf.

12. *Deep Listening* podcast #061, "The Myth of Multi-tasking: Working Memory and Listening with Professor Stefan van der Stigchel," oscartrimboli.com/podcast/061.

13. Uri Hasson, "This Is Your Brain on Communication," TED Talk, February 2016, ted.com/talks/uri_hasson_this_is_your_brain_on_communication.

Chapter 4: Hear, See, and Sense

1. *Deep Listening* podcast #070, "Teaching the World to Listen with Dame Evelyn Glennie," oscartrimboli.com/podcast/070.

2. *Deep Listening* podcast #020, "Understand the Art and Science of Listening: Cam Hough Explains the Maths of Sound in a Concert Hall and in an Office," oscartrimboli.com/podcast/020.

3. Sue Shellenbarger, "Just Look Me in the Eye Already," Quantified Communications, May 29, 2013, quantified.ai/blog/wsj-just-look-me-in-the-eye-already.

4. *Deep Listening* podcast #062, "How to Get Your Kids to Listen, with Dr. Justin Coulson," oscartrimboli.com/podcast/062.

5. *Deep Listening* podcast #092, "How to Effectively Listen to Someone Who Is Suicidal," oscartrimboli.com/podcast/092.

6. Paul Ekman, "Universal Facial Expressions," PaulEkman.com, paulekman.com/resources/universal-facial-expressions.

7. *Deep Listening* podcast #066, "Listening to Body Language with Susan Constantine," oscartrimboli.com/podcast/066.

8. *Deep Listening* podcast #042, "How to Listen across Generations," oscartrimboli.com/podcast/042.

9. *Deep Listening* podcast #083, "The Secrets of Listening for Emotions in the Workplace with Professor Marc Brackett," oscartrimboli.com/podcast/083.

10. *Deep Listening* podcast #036, "How to Listen like a High Court Judge with Justice Michael Kirby," oscartrimboli.com/podcast/036.

11. *Deep Listening* podcast #065, "Listen like World Memory Champion Dr. Boris Konrad," oscartrimboli.com/podcast/065.

Chapter 5: Explore the Backstory

1. *Deep Listening* podcast #095, "Three Practical Ways to Listen When You Disagree Fiercely—Simon Greer," oscartrimboli.com/podcast/095.

2. *Deep Listening* podcast #076, "Your Listening Is, at Best, a Wonderful Guess—Tracey Thompson and Mark Bowden," oscartrimboli.com/podcast/076.

3. Don Van Natta, "Serena, Naomi Osaka and the Most Controversial U.S. Open Final in History," ESPN, August 17, 2019, espn.com.au/tennis/story/_/id/27408140/backstory-serena-naomi-osaka-most-controversial-us-open-final-history.

4. *Deep Listening* #042, "Generations."

Chapter 6: Notice How It Is Said

1.   *Deep Listening* #092, "Suicidal."

2.   *Deep Listening* podcast #005, "Michael Henderson, Corporate Anthropologist, Outlines Why Most Employee Engagement Surveys Are Question Biased Rather Than Listening Optimised," oscartrimboli .com/podcast/005.

3.   *Deep Listening* podcast #081, "How to Easily Listen for When People Lie to You, with Chase Hughes," oscartrimboli.com/podcast/081.

4.   *Deep Listening* podcast #027, "Listen across Cultures and Continents: Tom Verghese Stresses the Importance of Understanding Your Culture before You Start to Listen to Other Cultures," oscartrimboli.com/ podcast/027.

Chapter 7: Focus On What Is Unsaid

1.   *Deep Listening* podcast #044, "Why Your Doctor Needs to Listen Deeply," oscartrimboli.com/podcast/044.

2.   Andrea Thompson, "Speed of Thought-to-Speech Traced in Brain," *Live Science*, October 16, 2009, livescience.com/5780-speed-thought -speech-traced-brain.html.

3.   *Deep Listening* podcast #028, "Vanessa Oshima Explains What Market Research Can Teach Us about Listening to Customers," oscartrimboli .com/podcast/028.

4.   *Deep Listening* podcast #086, "How to Effectively Listen to Someone's Voice," oscartrimboli.com/podcast/086.

5.   *Deep Listening* podcast #046, "Listen to Your Audience like sxsw," oscartrimboli.com/podcast/046.

6.   *Deep Listening* #028, "Vanessa Oshima."

7.   *Deep Listening* podcast #085, "Hidden Secrets of How to Listen for Non-Verbals," oscartrimboli.com/podcast/085.

Chapter 8: Listen for Their Meaning

1. *Deep Listening* podcast #030, "How Radical Listening Created a Global
    $175-Million Legacy: Kathy LeMay Explores the Impact of Listening
    and Not Pitching in the Not for Profit Sector," oscartrimboli.com/
    podcast/030.

2. *Deep Listening* podcast #049, "Curing Cancer with Listening Rather
    Than Chemotherapy: Dr. Bronwyn King," oscartrimboli.com/
    podcast/049.

3. *Deep Listening* podcast #007, "Listen like a Mediator: World-Class
    Mediator and Author of 37 Books on the Topic of Resolving Conflict—
    Ken Cloke Explores the 5 Levels of Listening," oscartrimboli.com/
    podcast/007.

4. *Deep Listening* podcast #001, "Jennifer MacLaughlin Shares
    How Auslan and Non-Verbal Speaking Helps Her Have Deeper
    Conversations," oscartrimboli.com/podcast/001.

5. Douglass P. Brazy, *Group Chairman's Factual Report of Investigation,
    Cockpit Voice Recorder DCA09MA026*, National Transportation Safety
    Board Vehicle Recorder Division, docket no. SA-532, exhibit No. 12,
    April 22, 2009, ntsb.gov/_layouts/NTSB/OpenDocument.aspx?
    Document_DataId=40314365&FileName=Cockpit%20Voice%20
    Recorder%2012%20-%20Factual%20Report%20of%20Group%20
    Chairman-Master.pdf.

6. *Deep Listening* podcast #087, "How to Effectively Listen to Autism
    Spectrum," oscartrimboli.com/podcast/087.

Over to You

1. John Stevens, *The Way of Judo: A portrait of Jigoro Kano and His
    Students* (Shambhala, 2013).

Acknowledgments

Writing a book about listening started with a question from Ingrid on July 2020. She said, "I googled the topic and wondered if you would be interested in writing another book."

Over the coming months, I invited a range of perspectives to understand how a book on this topic would advance and help others.

Practicing what I teach, I asked my clients, the Deep Listening Ambassadors and Community of Practice, and my editor about creating a comprehensive book about listening in the workplace. Then I asked a few peer authors who understand my work yet are dispassionate enough to tell me the truth. And, finally, I spoke to three publishers.

Exploring what was unsaid, I asked two thousand people who didn't know me for their thoughts too. I used qualitative and quantitative research to explore what they struggle with when listening in their workplace.

Next, we asked for feedback on the book title, the structure, and a range of chapters. As many as ninety-two people provided chapter-level feedback. Thanks to each of you for your thorough, thoughtful, and honest perspectives during this time.

The process of peer review drew on an incredible range of listening professionals from around the globe, who critiqued the content from an academic and practitioner perspective. Thanks to Avi Kluger, Jane Adshead-Grant, Katherine Tulpa, and Paul Lawrence.

I have enormous gratitude to two amazing research analysts who helped with finding the listening stories: Anit Girgla and Thomas Phillips. Each, in their unique way, challenged me to explore listening through the centuries, cultures, and continents.

They say it takes a village to raise a child and a tribe to create a book. I would like to acknowledge the great tribe that I am lucky to be a member of.

To Michaela, for your constant, daily professional support. You anticipate what's next and protect my time to make sure I reach the milestones I commit to for my clients, community, readers, and listeners.

There is a range of people who support the quest toward 100 million Deep Listeners in the world.

To Andrew Lewy, Barry Gibson, Bayu Sadewo, Brett Bannerman, Erik K. Johnson, Heidi Martin, Jane Wixon, Janika Barnes, Jessica Rhodes, Jill Covitz, Jonny McNee, Kellie Riordan, Lisa Catto, Luke Cook, Monique Ross, Maria Tickle, Melissa Prichard, Matthew Morrison, Monika Stelzner, Nell Norman-Nott, Steve Austen, Sarah Bishop, and Tammy Vigh: you each have played a vital role in assessment software, graphics podcast production, research, websites, and so much more.

To the more than one hundred guests who contributed your expertise in creating an award-winning podcast.

To over 150 newspaper journalists and podcast, radio, and TV hosts who have been open to sharing the Deep Listening message with their audience.

In the practice of being a better listener, I hold myself to the standards taught and role-modeled to me by Charity Becker, Hilary Armstrong, John Raymond, Mandy Geddes, Raquel Ark, Roma Gaster, and Vanessa Fudge. Thank you for setting and maintaining the standard.

I am fortunate enough to be part of a community of peers who orbit in a similar galaxy to me, yet at different seasons and via their unique paths. These trusted peers have the perspective to be professionally curious and ethically direct when I am stuck. I am grateful to call Amy Silver, Belinda Brosnan, Bryan Whitefield, Charlie Pidcock, Dave Stachowiak, Dermot Crowley, Digby Scott, Donna McGeorge, Gabrielle Dolan, Kelly Windle, Leanne Hughes, Jane Anderson, Janine Garner, Matt Church, Pete Cook, Tracey Ezard, and Zoe Routh. Your empathy and compassion for your clients and their outcomes inspire me to be better each day.

To the team at Page Two Books: thank you for listening. Although I spoke to three publishers, only one listened to me and what I craved for the readers and listeners of this book. Your passion, practicality, persistence, and professionalism throughout this process have created an artifact worthy of the quest for 100 million Deep Listeners in the world. Thanks to Amanda Lewis, Jennifer Lum, Kendra Ward, Melissa Edwards, Madison Taylor, Meghan O'Neill, Peter Cocking, Rony Ganon, and Trena White, who each played a vital role in bringing this book into the world.

Thanks to my clients for your enduring patience when I announce I want to experiment with something new; you are always open to the invitation and I appreciate your sense of humor.

To my editor, Kelly Irving, for your ability to notice when I am chasing blue rabbits and get me back to my responsibilities—you, the reader. Throughout this process, you have been endlessly patient and continuously encouraging, and you helped me to listen to myself.

It takes a particular skill to simplify the noise in my mind and mouth and create something that will be read, understood, and bring about a change. Thanks for taking the time to listen on behalf of readers and listeners.

Finally, to my wife, Jennie—the best listener I know. Thank you for your constant encouragement and thoughtful questions, and for listening to what I haven't said. Your belief in others helps them listen to themselves and to what matters and means the most to them.

About the author

Oscar Trimboli is an author, host of the Apple award-winning podcast *Deep Listening*, and a sought-after keynote speaker. He is passionate about using the gift of listening to bring positive change in homes, workplaces, and cultures worldwide.

Through his work with chairs, boards of directors, and executive teams, Oscar has experienced firsthand the transformational impact leaders can have when they listen beyond words.

He believes that leadership teams need to focus their attention and listening on building organizations that create powerful legacies for the people they serve—today and, more importantly, for future generations.

Oscar is a marketing and technology industry veteran with over thirty years of experience across general management, sales, marketing, and operations for Microsoft, PeopleSoft, Polycom, and Vodafone. He consults with organizations including American Express, AstraZeneca, Cisco, HBSC, Google, IAG, Montblanc, Microsoft, PwC, Salesforce, Sanofi, SAP, and Siemens.

He is also the head of the coaching faculty for the Marketing Academy Australia, where he supervises thirty executive coaches and their coaching engagements with thirty of Australia's highest potential marketing leaders during their immersive nine-month leadership development program. He is uniquely placed to understand the current challenges for brands, agencies, and customers.

In his spare time, Oscar loves his afternoon walks with his wife, Jennie, and their dog, Kilimanjaro. On the weekends, you will find him playing Lego with one or all of his four grandchildren.

oscartrimboli.com

Bring *How to Listen* into your organization

Since 2015, over 25,000 busy managers have accessed practical tools for workplace listening. What if your managers and leaders could regain one hour each day in their schedule through deeper listening?

What would that mean for your employees, your customers, your suppliers, your stakeholders, your policy outcomes, and your profitability?

The simplest way to make progress is to purchase *How to Listen* for all of the executives, leaders, and managers in your organization. When you purchase *How to Listen* across your organization, you will gain access to a range of practical tools and programs to sustain your team's learning beyond the book. These include the listening challenge and a range of thirty-minute embedding workshops that can be delivered across teams, departments, and divisions.

We can tailor the listening assessment for cohort specific reporting, giving you a tool for immediately assisting leaders to notice their listening barriers and, more importantly, what to do about it.

We offer a range of resources that can help you move your listening from awareness to skill and toward a practice.

The resources are all available at **www.oscartrimboli.com/ howtolisten**, or contact us directly at **hello@oscartrimboli.com**.